"Charles Denko is an excellent role model who overcame formidable obstacles—poverty and heart-wrenching polio— with Herculean initiative."

—Charles H. Grace, attorney, engineer, writer

"This is a good book about a very good man. It presents an image of a humble man who can inspire us all—the kind of person who gives us hope that we might have a chance to reverse the deterioration of values that is following the current wave of thoughtless human greed."

—William J. Cashman, former editor and publisher, *Beaver Beacon*

EARLIER BOOKS

The Psychiatric Aspects of Idiopathic Hypoparathyroid-
ism: Case Report and Survey of the World Literature
(under Joanne D. Denko, M.D. and Rudolf Kaelbling, M.D.)

Through the Keyhole at Gifted Men and Women:
A Study of 159 Members of the Mensa Society
(under Joanne D. Denko, M.D.)

A Handful of Ashes: One Mother's Tragedy
(under Victoria C. G. Greenleaf, M. D.)

Fighting the Good Fight: One Family's Struggle Against
Adolescent Alcoholism (under Victoria C.G. Greenleaf, M. D.)

Into a Mirror and Through a Lens: Forty Poems on the
Mother/Child Relationship from Conception to Marriage
(under Victoria C.G. Greenleaf, M. D.)

Interlink: and Other Nature/Humankind Poems
(under Victoria C.G. Greenleaf, M. D.)

Envy: A Survey of Its Psychology and History
(under Victoria C.G. Greenleaf, M. D.)

The Life of Charles W. Denko, Ph.D., M.D
(under Joanne D. Denko, M.D, M.S.)

A Quiet Hero

The Life of
Charles W. Denko, Ph.D., M.D.

Joanne D. Denko, M.D., M.S.

Cypress House

A Quiet Hero
The Life of Charles W. Denko, Ph.D., M.D.
Copyright © 2017 by Joanne D. Denko, M.D., M.S.

Cypress House
155 Cypress Street
Fort Bragg, CA 95437
800 773-7782
www.cypresshouse.com

Cover and book design by Mike Brechner/Cypress House
Cover Photograph by Bachrach Photographers, Holliston, Massachusetts
Photo credits:
Photos of Charles Denko and family, courtesy of Denko Family archives
Arcadia, page xiv, with permission from Heritage-Ships.com
Arthritic hands, page 64, © iStock.com/iMay
Platypus, page 76, © iStock.com/ David Bukach
Photo, page 126, by Diana McNees, reprinted with permission
from *The Plain Dealer*
Quotation from *The Structure of Evolutionary Theory* by
Stephen Jay Gould. Copyright © 2002 by the
President and Fellows of Harvard College.

PUBLISHER'S CATALOGING-IN-PUBLICATION DATA

Names: Denko, Joanne Decker, 1927- author.

Title: A quiet hero : the life of Charles W. Denko, Ph.D., M.D. / Joanne D. Denko.

Other titles: Life of Charles W. Denko, Ph.D., M.D.

Description: First edition.| Fort Bragg, CA : Cypress House, [2017] | Abridged version for young adults of: The life of Charles W. Denko, Ph. D., M.D. (Cypress House, c2013).

Identifiers: ISBN: 978-1-879384-00-2 | LCCN: 2015956929

Subjects: LCSH: Denko, Charles W., 1916-2005. | Physicians--United States--Biography. | Physicians--United States--Personal narratives. | Rheumatologists--United States--Biography. | Young adults--Conduct of life. | Teenagers--Conduct of life. | LCGFT: Biographies. | BISAC: JUVENILE NONFICTION / Biography & Autobiography / General.

Classification: LCC: R154.D46 D46 2017 | DDC: 610.92--dc23

First edition
Printed in the USA
2 4 6 8 9 7 5 3 1

To the memory of Charles's parents, Vassily and Evdokiya, and teachers, particularly A. K. Anderson, Ph.D., his mentor and friend, who encouraged his education, and to Charles J. Malemud, Ph.D., his colleague and friend, who supported Charles in his life work, this book is lovingly dedicated.

— Joanne D. Denko

"Good morning, fellow students."

—Charles Denko, every lecture worldwide

CONTENTS

Our theatrical and literary standards recognize only a few basic types of heroes. Most are preeminently strong and brave; some, in an occasional bone thrown to the marginal world of intellectuals, may even be allowed to triumph by brilliance.

—Stephen Jay Gould, *The Structure of Evolutionary Theory*

A Quiet Hero

"Work hard at something you love."

—Charles W. Denko

FOREWORD

When I considered that the life of my late husband, Charles Denko, could and should be an inspiration to young people, I decided that the way to accomplish this would be to prepare a shortened form of a biography I had already published, *The Life of Charles W. Denko, Ph.D., M.D.*

This is that book. *A Quiet Hero* omits the technical description of Charles's contributions to rheumatology, including several sections by his colleague and friend, Charles Malemud, Ph.D.; his curriculum vitae, his bibliography, and a timeline of his life.

I wrote that biography in a style I devised, never having encountered a biography so written. I had asked sons, a nephew, a niece, a lifelong friend and colleague (Malemud), and others to write vignettes about Charles from their individual perspectives. I intended this approach to present a multi-ocular vision of this remarkable, many-faceted man, to supplement the memories of his wife and companion of many years.

Included also in that biography are a number of vignettes by Charles himself, when, although in decline, he still helped me in any way he could. Since the biography was intended mainly for the grandchildren, some of whom had never known him, but those who did, only from the vantage of a child, it was supplemented with anecdotes from their elders. A few of these I have been able to include here.

Including material written by the subject himself, his biography is indexed under both biography and autobiography.

I hope you will enjoy reading about the fulfillment this scientist/physician/husband and father found in his life of service.

Joanne D. Denko

WE THINK OF HEROES as extraordinary people in extraordinary situations, like a firefighter who rescues tenants from a burning apartment building, a pilot safely landing a disabled airplane and saving the passengers, and a taxicab driver who delivers a baby, then baby and mother to the hospital. These people are certainly heroes, but there is another kind of heroism rarely mentioned in the news or on the Internet—the quiet hero.

Every hero shares the same attributes of courage under adversity and sacrifice for another's well-being. Quiet heroes are not flashy. Their achievements come from years of working to make people's lives better, often without reward or recognition. We depend on the quiet heroes as much as we do on those who risk their lives to save others. What both have in common is that they ask the question "What can I do to make life better?" One quiet hero in the field of medicine is Charles W. Denko, biochemist, physician, medical researcher, husband, and father.

When I asked my grandchildren (Madeleine, age 12, and Charles, age 9) to think of a hero they knew, Charles piped up, "Papa Chuck!" and his mother showed me a poem he had written in day camp about a hero:

> *He died when I was two,*
> *But he played make-believe*
> *Tea party with Madeleine.*
>
> —*Joanne D. Denko*

S/S *Arcadia*, Hamburg America Line.
Peninsular & Oriental Steam Navigation Company
steamship built 1888 by Harland & Wolff at Belfast.

Wasil and Evdokiya with Charles and Munya,
two immigrants and two first-generation Americans.

CHAPTER 1

CHARLES'S FOREBEARS AND EARLY EDUCATION (1916–1930)

CHARLES WAS BORN in poverty, and heard only Russian spoken. At age one he was stricken with polio. These circumstances shaped him, but did not deter him from becoming a medical research scientist respected throughout the Western world. His story has lessons for us all. He followed the best of his own advice: "Work at something important, and love it."

Almost at the border of Poland, near the city of Brest, is the town of Kobrin in the Russian province of Byelorussia (now Belarus). Byelorussia means "White Russia," and two explanations are given for its name. One is that it is derived from the people with a mixture of Swedish blood from the blond Swedes who invaded the Bug River (pronounced "Boog") along the Polish border. The alternative theory holds that "White Russia" comes from their traditional dress of white shirts or tunics with red trim.

In the fifteenth or sixteenth century, envoys from the court of Moscow invited Byelorussia to become part of Greater Russia. People in white tunics greeted the envoys and, as was their custom, scattered salt and bread as symbols of welcome. Byelorussia accepted the offer.

Charles's father, Vassily (Wasil) Denyko, was born in Byelorussia near the end of the nineteenth century. The family's land would not support three brothers, so the eldest remained on the farm, the second joined the army, and money was scraped together to send Wasil to the New World. He traveled across Europe through Hungary to the shipping docks at Hamburg, Germany, to board the *Arcadia** for the promise of America.

The *Arcadia* steamed across the Atlantic Ocean at thirteen knots (approximately fifteen miles per hour) with twenty first-class and 1,100 third-class passengers. Third class was referred to as steerage, where hopeful immigrants were squeezed together to breathe bad air and eat worse food served from enormous pots. Only first-class passengers enjoyed the journey and were allowed to stroll the decks in fair weather. Wasil knew the long voyage was over when he saw the Statue of Liberty holding her torch against the New York City skyline on January 13, 1909.

Before landing at the city docks, all the expectant immigrants had to be processed through the vast redbrick main building on Ellis Island. The immigration officer highhandedly changed Wasil's name to Charles and shortened Denyko to Denko. As he slept on the docks his first night, someone stole his paltry supply of rubles. Wasil quickly found farm work in

---

* In the full biography I quoted a family story that was erroneous. Charles had told me that his father was on the *Carpathia,* a ship that went to the rescue of the *Titanic.* I do not know how the error entered in, but I do not believe that either Wasil or Charles propagated a lie. *JD*

New York State and worked his way across Pennsylvania to Cleveland. With his powerful muscles, he found employment in the booming steel industry that later supplied the raw material for World War 1.

Evdokiya was an orphan girl in Byelorussia. After the death of her mother, she was sent to live with an uncle and worked on a neighbor's farm. A Russian Orthodox priest helped arrange her journey to America, and Evdokiya's employer sold a cow to raise the money for her ocean passage. She left her village of Antapol, near Brest, in 1914 and sailed on the last ship leaving Tsarist Russia before World War 1 began.

Unable to speak or read English, sixteen-year-old Evdokiya traveled alone across the Atlantic to Baltimore. As happened with Wasil, the immigration officer had trouble pronouncing her name and changed it to Anna for admittance into the country. Evdokiya rode the train from Baltimore to Cleveland, where the priest had found work for her as a maid and cook for a Jewish family that owned a bakery.

Like millions of others Wasil and Evdokiya came to America in search of a better life. The Statue of Liberty that Wasil saw in New York Harbor had on its base a sonnet by Emma Lazarus, "The New Colossus."

> Not like the brazen giant of Greek fame,
> With conquering limbs astride from land to land;
> Here at our sea-washed, sunset gates shall stand
> A mighty woman with a torch, whose flame
> Is the imprisoned lightning, and her name
> Mother of Exiles. From her beacon-hand
> Glows worldwide welcome; her mild eyes command
> The air-bridged harbor that twin cities frame.
> "Keep, ancient lands, your storied pomp!" cries she

With silent lips. "Give me your tired, your poor,
Your huddled masses yearning to breathe free,
The wretched refuse of your teeming shore.
Send these, the homeless, tempest-tossed to me,
I lift my lamp beside the golden door!"

Cleveland needed laborers for its steel mills, and many Eastern European immigrants were attracted by the availability of work. Wasil and Evdokiya met and were married on Halloween 1915 under the thirteen copper domes of the Saint Theodosius Russian Orthodox Cathedral, which the Czar of Russia helped build, and to which he donated the magnificent chandelier.

Their first child, Charles, was born August 12, 1916. Evdokiya did not like Cleveland, which she found loud, bustling, and dirty, so Wasil investigated other steel towns. They moved to Ellwood City, Pennsylvania, for its seamless tube mill and its woods and rolling hills in the foothills of the Appalachians. Nearby Connoquenessing Creek had a rock-protected inlet, relatively safe for swimming. The surroundings were greener and the steel-mill pay much better than in Cleveland. A friend of Wasil's owned a nearby farm where the couple sometimes helped with farm work and enjoyed picnics.

Evdokiya and Wasil's new family in the new land were faced with an old problem: Polio, or poliomyelitis, struck thousands of children in the United States until Dr. Jonas Salk's and Dr. Bruce Sabin's achievements of two different polio vaccines. In 1917, the infant Charles was one of the 27,363 reported cases. The disease came from contaminated food and water, especially milk. Many people recovered without permanent damage, but the virus that attacked Charles left him with damage that stopped messages from the nerves to the muscles. His mother and father did what they could to fight the disease.

They kept him in bed and placed hot water bottles on his legs to ease the pain. Charles survived with a shortened left leg, which made walking difficult and painful.

Other children were born into the Denko family: Munya (Eastern European for Mary), Helen, Ivan (John), and two later boys, Peter and Andrew. Andrew died in infancy, and Peter was born with a congenital heart lesion and died in early adult life. (It is ironic that just as Charles was born forty years too soon to benefit from polio prevention, his brother was born twenty-five years before Drs. Blalock and Taussig developed surgery for congenital heart abnormalities at the very medical school Charles and I were attending.)

Because of his responsibilities for his growing family, Wasil had to relinquish his hopes of attending night school to learn English. In 1925, he built the family home on an enormous lot. Evdokiya worked very hard to keep the house and raise the children, while Wasil did most of the gardening, after his factory work. Besides vegetables, there were apple, pear, sour cherry, and peach trees.

Evdokiya was like a mother tiger when it came to defending her children. A neighborhood girl teased and taunted Charles about his crippled leg. Evdokiya tried to reason with the girl's mother without success. Angry over the mother's failure to restrain the child, Evdokiya poured a panful of dirty dishwater from an upstairs window onto the head of the woman walking below. Evdokiya was taken to court and fined $10. She said, "The satisfaction was worth ten dollars," and Charles had no more problems from the child. (Ten dollars was a lot of money at that time.)

Charles's education began in the primary school close to his home in Ellwood City. Evdokiya went with him at a time when walking was still a struggle and painful for him. This was before school buses, and the family did not have a car. She took along a neighbor, a young woman fluent in Russian and English, to serve as interpreter for the procedures of attending school. In the family only the father spoke fluent though ungrammatical English, but he was at work in the mill, whereas the mother spoke only Russian. She needed to know the days and times Charles should arrive at school.

That year a dedicated first grade teacher immediately recognized Charles as gifted and devised special assignments for him to speed his learning of English. She was so successful that Charles entered second grade speaking perfect English without an accent.

Charles had the advantage of living in a small town where everyone knew each other. In his neighborhood most people were from Eastern Europe, so as a preschooler the first and only language sounds he heard were Russian, Polish, Ukrainian, etc. However once he was old enough to get around town on his own, many people noticed this intelligent, curious, polite, friendly boy with motivation to help himself and did whatever they could to help him. The Orthodox priest heard about him and came over to get him to religion classes. The Stevenson family, whose father was the Presbyterian minister, with children older and younger than Charles, included him in family events and outings. Their interest helped acculturate him and expand his English vocabulary.

One afternoon, Charles, at eight, was playing with a neighborhood boy, Metheny Buzard, on the playground near the boy's home, but Charles had a severe and painful limp. A car stopped and the driver motioned for the children to come over to him. Mrs. Buzard, the conscientious mother of an only child, came out and questioned the man in friendly conversation. She quickly realized that he was a member of the local

Shriners chapter of businessmen, whose main project was to help needy children with orthopedic problems. He had spotted an opportunity to help while driving past when he noticed that Charles was unable to play actively because of his polio-damaged leg, but doing the best he could in adversity.

The Shriners is a fraternity founded in 1872. What began as a group of men getting together for fun and fellowship soon became a philanthropic organization dedicated to helping handicapped children. No orthopedic physician was available locally, so Mrs. Buzard helped get Charles to the University of Pittsburgh for their staff to evaluate him. The Shriners accepted his case for surgical treatment and physical therapy, and Charles was taken without his mother to their hospital in St. Louis, Missouri, where surgeons lengthened a shortened tendon, greatly improving his walk. He underwent physical therapy for several months and continued to improve.

Evdokiya came out to St. Louis to check on Charles, despite having to bring along three younger children (Helen, Ivan, and Peter) because there was no one to care for them. (Munya, just seven, was left to cook for her father.) The hospital staff taught Evdokiya how to continue Charles's physical therapy at home, which she did, with an occasional visit to the local physician. Without the Shriners' help Charles would have remained so handicapped that he could never have held a normal job.

In the 1920s, children rarely went to their parents for extras. A movie ticket cost ten cents and a stick of licorice another five. Charles bought newspapers at the print shop for three cents each and sold them for five cents to workmen leaving the mill after their shift. The remaining change went into his pocket for the next show.

The special treat in Ellwood City was the Klondike, a chocolate-covered bar of vanilla ice cream costing five cents. Occasionally, strawberry ice cream replaced the vanilla and entitled the lucky holder to a free bar.

Radio was the most popular source of entertainment and information, and Wasil decided to buy a console for the family. It stood next to the phonograph and played loud enough for everyone in the room to hear. The radio had a wide range that could pick up broadcasts from Muscatine, Iowa, and especially station KDKA in Pittsburgh.

Charles was not satisfied with only Pittsburgh and Muscatine. To maximize the benefits, the radio needed an aerial. The advantage of the aerial was that you could listen to stations across the country and around the world. To increase the number of stations, a wire needed to be strung from the Denko house to an obliging neighbor's.

One day in spring, friends gathered with their carpentry tools while Evdokiya prepared a lunch in the kitchen. The house electric wire furnished the power source and framework to support the aerial as it stretched from porch to porch. Since the wire crossed the alley, the work had to be approved by the city engineer.

Between school and suppertime, Charles listened to the adventures, dramas, and comedies on the radio. Only Dick Tracy could "trace crime to its lair and bring justice to triumph." He rounded up every Public Enemy Number One as fast as each new one appeared. The little chatterbox, Orphan Annie, wasn't nearly as good as Jack Armstrong, who was great at every sport, climbed mountains, and piloted planes. On Monday, Tuesday, Wednesday, and Thursday, Buck Rogers took listeners into the twenty-fifth century with rocket ships circling Jupiter, Saturn, Mars, and Venus. Chief Lone Wolf welcomed all the braves and princesses around a campfire, and Tarzan swung from the vines in darkest Africa to protect his lovely Jane. Charles wrote an essay about children's radio programs, printed in a Geneva publication.

Besides the serials, the radio offered music: big band, swing, folk, and best of all, classical. Helen had the chore of scrubbing the kitchen floor on Saturday afternoons and often complained that Charles never let her listen to popular music because he wanted the Metropolitan Opera. This was despite his lack of musical talent. In fact, in fifth grade, one class in the curriculum was children's chorus, but it was soon apparent that Charles had no singing ability. His teacher gave up and asked him just to move his lips but not emit any sound.

A year later, in the sixth grade, a musical contest was held to identify classical masterworks and name their composers. To practice, students in Elwood City's four elementary schools listened to a set of recordings. The first prize was a silver dollar and a raincoat (offered by a local men's store), very useful in the Pennsylvania rainy season. Charles won, and credit went to his teacher. While Charles had no musical ability, he did have a good memory.

The silver dollar paid for ten movie admissions and the raincoat kept him dry. His teacher added her own accolade: she altered the school dismissal order and gave Charles the position of leading the class out of school each day.

> *"Chance favors the prepared mind."*
>
> — Louis Pasteur
>
> Many instances of this truth are displayed in Charles's own choices. However, the most heart-warming example of life-changing benefit to him stems from the "prepared mind" of the Shriner who observed a plucky eight-year-old boy playing despite a painful limp.

CHAPTER 2

CHARLES IS CAPTIVATED BY SCIENCE (1930–1944)

AT ELLWOOD CITY HIGH SCHOOL, Charles excelled. Mr. Gills, his chemistry teacher, devised experiments to feed Charles's interests in life processes. The physics course was of less importance to him, but under the teaching of Helen Mathews, biology proved as satisfactory as chemistry. Her students worked with plants, watering and pulling weeds as needed, and with small animals such as tadpoles and frogs. In her course of general science Charles had to keep fish and plants balanced in a small aquarium, using only supplies available from the local five-and-ten-cent store. He had them as pets but also learned to care for their needs.

Other teachers influenced Charles: Mrs. Wilson in Latin, Miss Abraham in French, Mr. Caplan in Problems of Democracy, Mr. Wilson in geography. Few young people were pushed to complete high school during the Depression years of the 1930s. They had to be ambitious and motivated, and many attended over the objections of their parents who, with many mouths to feed, needed additional income. With the declaration of war on December 7, 1941, many dropped out to enlist. At a reunion luncheon that Charles sponsored many years later, one member told of returning to high school after the war, being discouraged by the math teacher, but having the French teacher visit his father to give him the impetus to return and graduate.

The same was true of students across the racial spectrum. Charles was friendly with students inside and outside his Russian ethnic group. This included Marvin, an African American who managed to buy a secondhand dump truck for odd jobs and deliveries. Sometimes he gave Charles a ride, and Wasil, well aware of Marvin's difficulties, would give his son a couple dollars to give Marvin for eight gallons of gas. Marvin went on to study law, making a living and helping his friends in need of legal assistance.

On the rare occasions they worked together, Wasil was known as "Big Charlie" and Charles as "Little Charlie." Wasil was a great hulk of a man who weighed about 200 pounds, while Charles was eager to work but did not have the muscles of a career manual laborer. Wasil considered his son's amateurish efforts worthwhile but hardly on his level. With his bad leg, Charles could never work with his father in the steel mill, although it had been Evdokiya's dream to pack two "buckets," one for each to take to work in the factory. Sometimes father and son would help on the farm of a friend of Wasil's from the old country. Wasil believed in the value of honest work.

Wasil had the equivalent of a third grade education in Russia under the czars, but was very intelligent and a talented problem solver. He served in many ways like a social worker, helping newcomers without knowledge of the language or culture find work and get established without allowing the locals to take advantage of the "greenhorns." He would let the men sleep on an old couch in the basement and shovel coal into the furnace to keep the house warm overnight, or help in the garden where he raised much of the family's food, or do odd jobs like painting around the house.

The Denko family went through the Great Depression with Wasil having only part-time work. Knowing he enjoyed an advantage with his muscles, he helped other workers at the steel mill when they fell behind, explaining, "That skinny Italian also has a family to feed." Wasil took Charles shopping with his little wagon to bring home food for the family. He learned how to be economical, by buying ends of lunchmeat at a reduced price. Charles was in college before he knew that cookies came round and unbroken.

Around the time he started high school Charles joined an informal organization of six to ten teenage boys in the same school year. No girls were permitted in the group. The boys gathered only for friendship. One advantage over an organization like the Boy Scouts was that the group did not have to worry over account books.

Food was the boys' major concern. Members did small jobs for the owners of the stores where their parents shopped, and sold scrap metal to the junk dealers from New Castle. Occasionally they joined the girls from school in selling packs of leaf lettuce, green onions, and carrots. The boys took turns preparing the food over campfires in the woods surrounding Ellwood City, and a new member with special talent for cooking fish was greatly appreciated.

During summer months they camped and went swimming. For Halloween they had a costumed group. One year they won the prize the city offered to those in the parade. They organized volleyball, mushball, horseshoe, and swimming teams to meet demands from playgroups such as little leagues.

Charles graduated from Ellwood City High School with the highest academic record and was named valedictorian. The Denko women had different views from the men on education as a preparation for life. Evdokiya, elder sister Munya, and younger sister Helen took the traditional view of their generation for women, i.e., finishing public high school was adequate education for life and work. Although both sisters were in the upper 10 percent of their classes, they did not accept their father's offer to help them in college as he had done for Charles and would later do for Ivan. They assumed their high school standing would get them clerical work in retail establishments, light factory work, or office work.

The state of Pennsylvania granted the winner of a competitive examination held every year in each county a four-year scholarship to any Pennsylvania college or university of the student's choice. Charles won and went to his chemistry teacher for help. The teacher recommended Geneva College in Beaver Falls, only ten miles from Ellwood City. The college was already known for its chemistry department, and a few years later Geneva received special accreditation from the American Chemical Society for its excellent chemistry education.

An added advantage of going to Geneva College was being close to home. Charles hitchhiked to school or shared driving expenses with other students. The state did not include any extras in the scholarship, and Charles earned what he needed for room and board by getting up at four in the morning to stoke the furnace in the boiler room at Geneva. Besides his main interests in chemistry and history, Charles took advantage of college geography courses, including social and economic geography. Charles thereby acquired an exceptional knowledge of the world. No one could ever beat him at Trivial Pursuit. His debate team beat Harvard's. He joined the archery team, a sport that depended on eyes and arms rather than legs.

When Charles was in college, his English professor, Don Wolfe, was preparing a four-year course in English, with one book for each year. Charles told me that Wolfe asked him to write sections on propaganda and debate. I have tracked down the series and found those sections, but they are without a byline. (I was surprised that the propaganda section did not, as I had expected, mention Joseph Goebbels, Hitler's minister of propaganda during the Nazi era. Several years later, the first mention I heard of propaganda was in connection with Goebbels.) However, both Charles (a budding chemist and a champion debater) and his friend Carl Zerke (I don't know his major) are credited in Wolfe's acknowledgments for reading and commenting on Wolfe's project. Zerke was Charles's friend who, forty years later, called Charles about his grandson's medical problem, which the physicians in Florida had not diagnosed or helped. Charles had Carl's wife, Bianca, bring the boy to Fairview Hospital, where Charles diagnosed scleroderma, began treatment, and later worked with the Florida pediatrician in the child's care. That patient, grown up, after his grandparents' death, wrote to Charles to thank him for his life-saving help.

Charles also announced sporting events on the town radio station and wrote news articles for the *Ellwood City Ledger.* In 1938 he received his Bachelor of Science degree in chemistry with high honor from Geneva College.

❋

Charles's next stop was graduate school at Pennsylvania State University, 170 miles from home in State College, Pennsylvania.

Evdokiya was very proud of her son. Accustomed to a language in which the adjective follows the noun, she told the milkman in broken English, "My boy's in the state pen." Penn State and the state penitentiary are only a few miles apart but very different in significance.

Once Charles came home on vacation to a quiet house. Evdokiya said, "I have a surprise for you. Munya, clear the table." A sheet of paper and a pen materialized. Charles was puzzled by his mother's strange behavior and wondered what was happening. She arranged the paper, took the pen, wrote, and handed the paper to him. The words were "Evdokiya Denko." She said, "Now I can sign any papers you want, the way you told me." But she never progressed in literacy beyond her name.

Charles received his Master of Science in organic chemistry in 1939, continuing his journey as a curious small-town boy facing an interesting future. He immediately began studies for his Ph.D. The initials stand for Doctor of Philosophy, but in the academic world "philosophy" means "love of wisdom."

He wanted to use his talents in the field of biochemistry, and solve the problems facing everyone, especially those of his mentor, A. K. Anderson, professor of physiology. Anderson suffered from rheumatoid arthritis. The cause of the disease was unknown, and it crippled, and continues to cripple, many of the people afflicted with it. The professor was already wheelchair-bound when Charles met him. One of Charles's jobs was writing Anderson's notes on the blackboard before class. Charles learned much under his guidance.

One day in his office the professor looked at Charles over his eyeglasses and asked, "Denko, do you want a good problem for your thesis work?"

Of course this was Charles's next step. He replied: "Yes, boss."

The professor's suggestion was new treatments for rheumatoid arthritis. He went on, "I think you can do it with animal models."

Anderson suggested that Charles work in Albert Bruce Sabin's (of oral polio vaccine fame later) Cincinnati laboratory during summer vacation to learn the principles of using animals in laboratory research. This would give him the experience he needed to continue his project at Penn State. He planned various aspects of the study and began working.

Intent on taking advantage of the cultural offerings at Penn State, Charles attended a series of lectures by notables the university brought in, and in some cases the receptions held for them. One such lecturer was Amelia Earhart, the first aviatrix to fly across the Atlantic, who later went down in the Pacific on the last leg of a round-the-world flight. She inspired an entire generation of women, and was a role model for many of my generation's mothers. Another visitor was the Russian composer, musician, and conductor Sergei Rachmaninov. On the occasion of his visit, the Russian professor, who was also a Russian Orthodox priest, invited his students (Charles was studying literary Russian) to a special reception to meet and speak with this Russian native speaker, who spoke little or no English. Other notables whom Charles met included Walter Hampden, an actor, and Robert Frost, poet of New England, and from 1958 to 1959 our country's poet laureate.

❋

For male students at Penn State and other colleges and universities, the phrase "my war years" began with a drawing of numbers that represented every birthday of the year. To supply manpower for the war effort, local draft boards were designated to select conscripts with the fairness of chance, so one beautiful summer day, a large fishbowl was filled with slips of paper with numbers corresponding to all the days of the year.

Each month another number was drawn. Having your birthday called meant you were drafted into the armed forces to fight in World War 2, with no designated endpoint, and returning home depended on the duration of the war. Those with the highest numbers would be called up last—perhaps never.

Charles lived in an apartment with three other chemistry graduate students (Iz, Murray, and Cy), and one held number 156 (birthday in early June). This made him eligible for the first call-up. However, students majoring in chemistry were declared essential for the war effort and could not be drafted. Enlisting was not unheard of, but faculty advisors suggested that the graduate students would benefit their country more by first finishing their coursework. Charles was automatically deferred because of his shortened leg.

When Charles was a year into writing his thesis, the supervisory committee felt the title, *Synthesis of Organo-Gold Compounds and a Study of their Biochemical Effects in Rats*, did not fit, so Charles added a pharmacology section with useful information about the treatment of rheumatoid arthritis. Undesirable side effects appeared in Charles's study. Gold caused kidney failure in rats, as it sometimes did in human patients. Eventually Charles found a way to reduce the danger by starting with a small dose. By keeping close track of their patients' kidneys, doctors could reduce the damage caused by treatment.

Shortly before Charles left Penn State, *The New York Times*, noted for its science coverage, sent a reporter to central Pennsylvania to interview Charles and Anderson, and an article appeared about their work. It is unusual for a major newspaper to show this kind of interest in a graduate student's work in another state.

Charles persuaded the university to accept Russian and French as his Ph.D. requirement for two foreign languages. The rest of the candidates used French and German. He argued that good chemistry papers were coming out of the USSR. His thesis was accepted and Charles at twenty-seven received his Ph.D. in physiologic chemistry in 1943.

Charles W. Denko, valedictorian.
(Voted the most humorous man in his class.)

Captain Denko, US Army.

CHAPTER 3

CHARLES REUNITES JEWISH ORPHANS WITH RELATIVES AND PREVENTS A PHONY DRUG FRAUD (1945–1947)

THE SUMMER AFTER GRADUATION Charles taught chemistry at West Virginia University in Morgantown. Soon thereafter he was hired as a research chemist at SMA Research Laboratories, Wyeth Institute of Applied Biochemistry, in Chagrin Falls, Ohio. Several months later an army recruitment officer came to the lab looking for a chemist. Charles persuaded him that despite his shortened leg, he qualified for several military specialties. He was offered a place on the Manhattan Project, highly secret work leading to the atomic bomb. Although he would have been useful doing the kind of work they needed, he avoided this prestigious assignment, explaining that his was the "wrong kind of chemistry." His interest and training were in the chemistry of the body in health and disease. Wishing to continue what he had been trained to do instead of taking a glamorous secret assignment illustrates his heroic qualities of lifelong service. The officer offered him a commission as first lieutenant in the Sanitary Corps, which he joined in January 1945.

When the time came to put his religion on his dog tags, instead of C(atholic), P(rotestant), or J(ewish) he had them mark his tags "RO" for Russian Orthodox, which was another first. Charles was sent to a training camp at Carlisle Barracks in Carlisle, Pennsylvania, where he spent five weeks in the 80th Officers Training Battalion. He and the other officers-in-training were taught much that was useful throughout life, not just while in the army.

In cooking class, they learned that using KP (kitchen patrol) as punishment yielded a poor nutritional result. Assigning personnel to food service as a specialty gave it status, kept the men well fed, and produced better morale. To assess results, class members stood at the end of the line where the men brought back trays and questioned them about the food being thrown out. One problem resulted from the kitchen personnel boiling large and small potatoes together for the same length of time, thus turning out large rocks mixed with mush. The problem was solved with a little instruction. A representative from Howard Johnson's Restaurants came to the Carlisle graduation and offered the officers jobs as restaurant managers when their tours of duty ended.

In another course they were taught principles of packing and shipping. They learned from an earlier mistake: airplane parts were sent to the war theater to be assembled onsite, but all the propellers were packed together and the ship carrying them was sunk. None of the planes could be completed until more propellers arrived.

Finally, the officers participated in war games with a mock battle and put Charles in charge of casualties. On his clipboard he listed three levels of injury according to severity: 1.

Fatal cases—pain medication only in the field; 2. Severe but salvageable—priority move to field hospital; and 3. Minor and less severely injured—later treatment. His instructors were astonished by the intelligent design of his plan.

In winter 1944 he began his first assignment by organizing the Army Medical Nutrition Laboratory in Chicago.

Charles considered himself (and was) an expert in nutrition. By this is meant something much broader than "diet" and closer to "metabolism." He was asked to study the long-term effects of army K rations, which he conducted on conscientious objectors, men who for religious reasons preferred not to fight but offered their bodies for research. For months these healthy young men ate the same monotonous diet given to service personnel assigned to active duty in the field. Studying their output (urine and feces), Charles found no damage to their health, and, with his staff members, wrote six papers documenting the studies. He was later grandfathered into the American Board of Nutrition as a diplomate as a result of these studies. After the war the value of his work was recognized by the Walter Reed Army Museum's request for a photograph for their collection of 400 medical scientists going back to Paracelsus in the sixteenth century. As late as the year 2000 a young woman accosted Charles in the hospital hall to inquire: "Are you the Dr. Denko who studied nutrition in conscientious objectors in World War 2? We study your papers in my nutrition class."

After years of terrible fighting (four for us, six for the other Allies and the Axis), the war had finally dragged to an end. The Allied powers of the United States, Britain, France, and the USSR had defeated the Axis of Germany, Italy, and Japan. The time had come to repair the damage and rebuild. More than any other victor in history, the U.S. was generous in offering a hand up to our erstwhile enemies, who had entangled us into the war when we were trying to stay neutral. Just as Herbert Hoover had made his fame (and later was elected president) by feeding Europe after World War 1, so our Marshall Plan sent food and other supplies, including medical, after World War 2. Within a few decades we saw an illustration on a national scale of an old adage: I know why that man hates me; I did him a favor.

Charles' service time had overlapped the end of the war and the beginning of the Occupation of Europe. Having finished his nutrition studies on healthy young men, he was assigned as a sanitation officer to serve in hungry and devastated Europe.

Wasil, Charles's father, like thousands of other Americans, was concerned about the fate of relatives abroad. News had come about a village where part of the Denyko family lived. The Germans had rounded up the villagers in a barn and set it afire. One young Denyko woman was spared because she happened to be visiting in another village that day. Knowing that many letters had not gotten to America during the war, relatives hastened to write to reassure their relatives or to convey the unhappy news, as the case might be.

There is a Russian film, *Come and See,* directed by Elem Klimov, showing this precise strategy, and indicating that over 600 villages suffered this fate. In *War and Peace*, Tolstoy's monumental novel set in the Napoleonic era, Napoleon's troops torched villages the same way and went on to burn Moscow.

Soon Wasil received a letter from his sister living in a village back home. The letter was posted from Dobrenichin, Byelorussia, a collective farm about fifty miles east of Brest. With the letter was a snapshot of several women, two elderly and three or four younger, and one young male. In her letter Wasil's sister explained that this was a family portrait of the remaining Denyko/Denko family. No one else was left. She explained that there were no other males in the family line due to the devastation of the war. Two women survived at collective farms. The writer said she was satisfied with food and housing. She felt well cared for. She was content.

Having completed his nutrition study about the time the war was ending, Charles then was stationed in New Jersey awaiting an army transport to take him to his next assignment in Europe. It was like being on furlough. He spent an occasional weekend with his friends, Walter and Nina Bouquet, from Ellwood City, who introduced him to others of Russian descent in the area. In the mid-twentieth century, Russian immigrants included both the poor like Charles's parents, former peasants who had come to the United States seeking opportunity and a better life, and the *nouveaux pauvre* (you've heard of the nouveaux riche), remnants of the tsarist aristocracy. They had escaped Communist bullets and fled from Russia ahead of the Bolsheviks with only the clothes on their backs, into which were sewn as many precious jewels as they could manage. Many drove taxis in Paris, and if you asked to be taken to the cathedral, you were let out not at Notre Dame but at the Russian Orthodox Cathedral with its world-famous choir. In the United States the émigrés clustered in New York City and maintained a subculture.

Charles's friends introduced him to Tanya, a graduate student in Russian. Her father was a professor of Russian at the University of Illinois at Urbana. When the United Nations center was established in New York City, Tanya's parents were employed as Russian translators. Tanya's father took Charles to a session at the Assembly when Nikita Khrushchev spoke. He used the Russian word *mir,* which has two meanings: "peace" and "world." On that occasion, the translator chose his unintended meaning. Khrushchev had banged his fist on the table and shouted, "We want peace," but was translated as saying, "We want the world." A near-riot broke out as the audience jumped up and ignored the Assembly police, to protest the second meaning, yelling, "They want the whole world!" Khrushchev himself was bellowing, "No! No! No!" When the chairman finally restored order, the error was corrected.

One day Charles called Tanya for an evening out. She invited him to a Christmas party, a gala evening hosted by her parents and friends, the former Russian nobility. As a young Russian-speaking American officer, Charles was welcomed and introduced to the personalities around the ballroom, many wearing the jewels and tiaras they had smuggled out of Russia and had not yet been forced to sell. The chambermaid who had made up Charles's room at the Plaza Hotel was a former duchess, and a handsome white-haired man was a count. Tanya explained that the partygoers did not want to exploit their former status. She introduced him to a tall elderly woman, Alexandra Tolstoy, the youngest of the novelist Leo Tolstoy's eleven children, whom he called by the Russian pet name Sasha. Sasha had prepared her father's novels on the wonderful new invention, the typewriter. She had managed to buy a vineyard with a motel along the Hudson, so her friends could visit and chat around the samovar as Russians like to do. She invited Charles, but his transport ship had arrived.

Sent to Europe to participate in the postwar cleanup, Charles was stationed at the 98th General Hospital in Munich. He had a variety of military duties. He worked as the border station inspector for refugees' health as they were brought from the Eastern Zone of occupation and were dusted with sulfa to prevent typhus.

As the Nazis swept through Poland, Byelorussia, and Czechoslovakia in the early years of the war, they took children with blond hair and blue eyes, usually Jewish, and sent them to Germany for adoption to be raised as Aryans. Once the youngsters were taken back to Germany, officers and other powerful people probably got the first choice, but those families were not engaged in a humanitarian act. Instead, childless couples took in the children to raise as good Germans, with no intention of giving them back to their rightful families. These children's existence was discovered at war's end because the Germans kept good records and the International Red Cross was given access to them. The children, between the ages of eight and twelve, were well dressed and clean, unlike the survivors of the concentration camps Charles saw.

Using the records as a map, the Red Cross located several hundred of the children, removed them from their German homes, and brought them to the displaced persons camps. An effort was made to group children from the same country or region, with the older ones trying to take care of the younger ones. One youngster was a little older and a little taller than the rest. He gathered his group of charges together and tried to comfort and reassure them. "We will be all right," he told them. The younger ones huddled under his arms and seemed to get strength from him.

Since Charles spoke "a little" German, Russian, French, and Polish and understood the children's problems, he was put in charge of supervising their return to their birthplaces. First, he had to persuade his superiors. The colonel was concerned that some of the children might be sick and said only the healthy ones should be repatriated, but Charles knew of a stronger medicine, the healing qualities of returning to one's own family. When the children were apprised of the planned repatriation, not one asked to go back to Germany.

The next hurdle was locating the missing families. In most

cases it was possible to identify and find the real families, rarely parents, given that 6 million Jews had perished in the Holocaust, but an aunt, a cousin, anyone within the child's extended family they could find. Charles was responsible for the return of at least thirty of the children.

The army had access to penicillin, the new miracle drug whose production involved fermentation in huge vats to grow the mold *penicillium* and then separation from the culture medium. The penicillin was then placed in vials that held one-half ounce and were capped with a rubber stopper. Lifesaving for these infections, the drug was used primarily for servicemen. The supply was limited, and was under control of the U.S. Army, which shared with the civilian population, particularly children suffering from meningitis and other infections to which they had little resistance resulting in part from poor diet. Many civilians died for lack of penicillin.

Officials learned that certain empty vials had significant value because of their prior use and labeling. Because it was in very short supply and in great demand, penicillin sold for $50 a vial on the black market. Deceitful black marketeers would sell penicillin diluted with tea, or else a fake mixture of the same amber color as that impure product, in those very recognizable vials, which they went through garbage dumps to find. Many people died from lack of genuine treatment. The diluted penicillin was even worse because there might be enough potency to save the life of a child but leave him or her with a damaged brain. (This cruel black-market activity is a central part of the novella and movie *The Third Man* by Graham Greene. The effect of the fake penicillin is illustrated more graphically in the British release than in the American.)

To combat this criminal and inhumane activity, Charles was sent under armed guard to keep the empty vials out of the hands of black marketeers. On the outskirts of Vienna where all the hospitals disposed of their trash, Charles dug through the piles of refuse until he found the used vials and smashed them. He never knew how many lives he saved.

Charles also went on sanitation and nutrition inspection tours of displaced persons camps. At one, he heard officials discussing a prisoner condemned to hang when the camp moved to Palestine. The man, who was accused of being an informant for the Nazis, believed he had not been given a fair trial. Charles questioned the officer in charge and found that the accusation had not been proven. He insisted on turning the accused over to the U.S. Army's Counterintelligence Division (CID).

Several weeks later, as Charles walked down a street in Salzburg, the man ran up to him, kissed his hand and arm, and wept in gratitude. So did his wife and daughter. The CID had investigated his case and determined he was not an informer. Another trial found him innocent and he was freed.

On a gloomy day in early spring Charles traveled from Munich to the massive blocks of dark stone of Landsberg Prison, where as a young man Adolf Hitler had been incarcerated for treason. Charles walked through puddles of melting snow and followed the signs directing visitors to the office of the commanding officer.

"What can I do for you, Captain?" asked the commandant, who recognized Charles's rank from his uniform.

"I'd like to visit Hitler's room."

"Fine. Follow me."

He led Charles down a long corridor and stopped before

an iron door set with iron bars. The commandant opened the squeaking door and they entered the small, sparsely furnished cell. He led Charles to the window and waved his arms at various buildings.

"Nothing to see here except prisoners," he said, but as they turned to go he added, "I have someone for you to see because you're in the medical field. Tomorrow will be too late."

They passed down several long corridors and stopped at last at the door of a large cell where a white-haired old man sat typing.

"*Kommen Sie hier, bitte,*" the commandant said. The old man kept typing.

Charles asked his guide who the man was.

"He is the world-famous tropical medicine specialist Claus Karl Schilling, here for medical war crimes. Every time a patient needs a blood count, he does it for us."

"What do you do then?"

"What would *you* do?"

"I'd check it."

"Exactly what we do."

"What is he famous for?"

"The test for diphtheria devised by this man helped millions, mostly children, in the past."

"Then what did he do that was criminal?"

"Under Hitler he performed infectious disease experiments on twins, that were not valid research anyway but resulted in both twins' death. He had the control twins killed too."

Charles questioned further: "What happens now?"

"He has an appointment with the gallows tomorrow."

On his way out, Charles noticed that the gallows had been freshly painted.

Later that year, Charles drove along a winding highway and spotted an attractive stone house, the centerpiece of a well-kept estate. Since he had no need to hurry, he turned off the highway, stopped at the front door, and rang the bell. A neatly dressed middle-aged woman asked, "*Was wünschen Sie?*"

He answered in the army version of the local dialect and soon established that the woman was Czech. Charles continued speaking in a mixture of Russian and German (*Amerikanischer deutsch*), filling in the words he did not know with gestures and pointing.

The woman told Charles the property had been the private home of a high-ranking Nazi leader, and Hitler was once a guest. Currently it served as a rest house for officers of the Occupation, and was used mainly on weekends and holidays.

"I see by your uniform that you are an American officer, and so the club is for you." She offered to show Charles around, where beautiful furnishings represented the life of the powerful. The woman showed him to the library and served him tea and cookies.

Charles thought of how he, the son of American immigrants, was sitting in the chair of a Nazi leader. He leafed through various volumes in the library.

"I see you are interested in books," she said. "I suggest you take a souvenir. Here is the one that Hitler used as an excuse to invade and conquer." She gave him a copy of the German book *Bavaria Leads the Push Toward the East* by Heinz Haushofer and Johann von Leers. It was inscribed "H. Himmler, April 1939."

⁂

Only by chance did Charles and Ivan arrive home on leave at the same time when Charles had a furlough from Europe and flew back. Except for family emergencies or death, service personnel were not granted leaves for family get-togethers. Ivan was serving in the U.S. Navy. They had put him through the University of Chicago Medical School and he later repaid the debt by time in the Public Health Service, covering Washington and Alaska, where he managed an epidemic. Evdokiya sat on the porch swing and said to Ivan and Charles, "I'm glad you could come home together this time."

She wanted to go shopping at Doude's, a small dry goods store, for emblems of the Denkos' patriotism. These were little flags with a blue star that many families with military personnel hung in their front windows. A gold star represented a death in the service.

Since they didn't have a car, Ivan and Charles spoke up quickly. "Mom, you don't need to walk downtown. We can get them and carry home whatever else you need."

"No, boys," she said. "Thanks anyway, but I want to carry the flags."

Her sons persisted until she explained, "You know that Mrs. Jones behind the counter. She tells me about her son and how he is a good officer. I want you to go with me. No other mother in town has two officer sons."

⁂

Back in Europe after his furlough, Charles was deployed to Berlin. Immediately after World War 2 the city had been divided into four sectors and governed by the US, France, USSR, and Britain. Deciding to visit the Soviet sector, Charles traveled by public transportation from his billet in West Berlin to a city park. Spring flowers and shrubbery with bright spots of yellow, red, white, and blue dotted a green background. In other areas a brown background showed where the public walked. Charles took his camera from a pouch and turned around for a good photo.

At that moment a Soviet major addressed him in Russian. "There are better scenes ahead." Charles responded in Russian, and the major tried to sell him a pair of binoculars. As they chatted, Charles told him his parents were from the city of Brest, a border town of 30,000 inhabitants, in Byelorussia. The major said that city was the site of his most recent campaign. He added, "The fighting was fierce." When the battle was over, the town was in the hands of the Soviet Army. This six-foot major described the destruction: "There was not a wall left standing as high as I am."

He was hospitable and invited Charles to his officers' club. He explained that the army was not paid as often during field campaigns as they were during garrison duty. The major had several thousand military rubles to spend, but only outside the USSR. Charles took directions to his club for a special social evening at army headquarters, while the major went looking for souvenirs.

That evening Charles returned to the Russian garrison. He crossed a busy street used mainly for pedestrians. The few motor vehicles slowed as he approached another imposing building. He recognized a group of USSR officers by their insignia. There were many generals, known as marshals in the Soviet rank. Several approached Charles, who explained that he had forgotten the name of the officer who had invited him to the officers' gala.

"Stop!" The loud order rang out in the dark night. The venue was the flower garden leading from the boulevard to a stone mansion the Soviet Army used for its administration of Berlin.

Charles knew enough Russian to halt when the armed sentry thrust his rifle forward and barked. Asked to state his business, Charles explained the invitation to the party from a Soviet fellow officer whose name he had forgotten but who had worked with him on the same detail as part of the Allied Occupation. (One such detail was a representative of each of the four Allied countries riding together around Berlin in an open Jeep.) The officer called his superior, who immediately arrived to give permission for Charles to attend.

The entertainment consisted of dancing, card playing, snacks and vodka, and a classical pianist. It was not at all rowdy but quiet and cultured. The women were smartly groomed. The star performer was the internationally known pianist Emil Gilels, who performed in a small theater seating several hundred. Gilels and the members of the small orchestra wore civilian clothes. Most of the men were in military dress. Charles was offered drinks, all alcoholic. No one invited him to play cards. He was free to wander around without being followed.

Charles mustered out as "U.S. Army (Captain) Nutrition Officer, Biochemist, Microbiologist, Sanitary Corps, United States and European Theater of Operations." He had been offered the rank of major as an inducement to stay.

"To be with family [relatives],
people like yourself…
is the best medicine."

—Captain Charles Denko

The Decker-Denko wedding.

"That's no girl... That's my wife!"

— Charles Denko's adaptation of an old joke

CHAPTER 4

TWO MEDICAL STUDENTS MARRY (1947–1951)

BY 1947, I HAD COMPLETED my undergraduate work at Hope College in Holland, Michigan, with a Bachelor of Arts with highest honors, the seventh in the history of the school to graduate with a 4.0 average. Delighted to be accepted at the world's premier medical school, Johns Hopkins University College of Medicine, I spent the summer having fun as a Student-in-Industry in Chicago and preparing to move to Baltimore to do whatever it would take to learn, develop, and transform myself from a premed at twenty into a physician at twenty-four.

In the spring Charles had returned from service in the army and by summer he had also been accepted at Johns Hopkins. The Servicemen's Readjustment Act, or G.I. Bill, Congress's landmark legislation, provided tuition and living expenses for veterans to pursue higher education. This act not only rewarded the veterans and swelled the middle class but also raised the country's skill and educational capital. Charles arrived in Baltimore in late August, having turned thirty-one on August 12. He was following his mentor's advice: "Denko, for the research you want to do, get your own M.D." At the time there seemed no possibility, but Charles was adept at seeing and seizing opportunities, and the GI Bill was exactly what he needed.

❋

At convocation we had been informed that with the influx of returning veterans, only one in seventeen applicants nationwide had been accepted to any medical school. There were eight women in our class of seventy-eight. The class included many veterans, several bringing wives and children. They told us also that, unlike most medical schools, Hopkins had not offered us a place in the class to flunk a certain percentage, a terrible waste of everyone's time and money. They had accepted us because they had confidence in us and intended to graduate all of us. If we had problems we were invited to seek help. This policy made medical school an unpressured (though intensive) pleasure.

One September evening the second-year students gave a mixer for the first-year students to get acquainted. At the party I noticed several things about Charles. He was the oldest member at thirty-one, the result of his being the only one with both a Ph.D. and service time. Several others had one or the other. We were sitting most of the time, and I didn't notice his limp. I picked up on the fact that he made a point to impress me with his credentials, i.e., his degree and his service time. I wondered why.

Immediately Charles began courting me. It was apparent he was not put off by anything he learned as we came to know each other better. He showed love by doing the little and big, kind and helpful things. He tolerated having my best friend, Iza, along with us for picnics, plays, and lectures at the Homewood campus and we were a compatible group. His car, an old Studebaker, took us anywhere Iza and I wanted to go. Once when we attended a performance in Washington, D.C., Iza and I fell asleep on the way back to Baltimore. Charles got lost and we were no help but would wake up every time he passed a certain doughnut factory, laugh, and go back to sleep. He invited me to dinner and the ballet because he knew I was appreciating my first chance to enjoy the cultural offerings of a big city. He too liked cultural events and told me what he had attended in Salzburg such as *Jedermann,* a medieval play performed on the steps of the cathedral.

As we progressed in medical school, we often drove to the oil refinery, where hundreds of lights twinkled against the night sky. We talked about our lives and plans for the future, and became truly acquainted. I learned of his interest and work in research at the School of Public Health at Hopkins. He was more than ready for marriage but I was still growing up.

I know how lucky I was, considering that in the mid-twentieth century intelligent women were taught to hide their brainpower because most men, including bright ones, considered intelligence their exclusive domain. I knew I needed a husband of high intelligence.

As medical school progressed, Charles and I had many opportunities to get to know each other because our rotations were determined alphabetically and my surname was Decker. We were one table apart on cadavers. Charles disliked anatomy and considered it a waste of time for someone not going into surgery. He failed anatomy the first year. After passing the test in the fall, he said, "I could have failed it again."

✻

At both Penn State and Hopkins, Charles was close enough to his hometown, Ellwood City, Pennsylvania, to get home for an occasional weekend. He told me about one visit from Penn State when he was met by Wasil at the door with an official-looking letter from the city. Charles saw that it pertained to the property his father had bought in the country and contained several legal phrases, which Charles did not want to try interpreting. Charles told him he should go to the union office or ask a lawyer friend of Charles's for an explanation.

"How many years have you been going to school?" Wasil asked.

Without inquiring why he asked, Charles quickly added up twelve through high school, four more of college, and yet another four of graduate school. "Twenty," he said.

"Twenty years?" Wasil repeated. "In Russia if we sent a *horse* to school twenty years, he'd know the answer."

(When I heard the story, I surmised what was coming, but Charles did not, due to his trusting nature.)

✻

As Charles told me about his family, he kept referring to "Ivan," pronounced the same as "Yvonne," until I finally asked how *she* was a *man*. About this time Ivan changed his name to its Anglicized equivalent, John. Charles attributed this idea to Gloria, John's wife. Madeleine, their eldest child, sent me copies of a collection of postcards and letters Charles had sent to "Ivan" while in the service, and the returns were signed "Ivan," but by the time I met him he was going by John. The youngest of the surviving children, John's life pattern resembled his brother's: First he enlisted in the navy, which put him the rest of the way through college and through the University of Chicago Medical School. Then he specialized in pathology, and later accepted an invitation to join Ralph Zientek, a classmate, in his pathology practice in Amarillo, Texas. Ralph died quite young, leaving John with the practice.

Finally we found ourselves in our third year. I still felt too young for the commitment of marriage, but Charles's patience was wearing thin. Knowing we were good friends and that I wanted the best for him, he asked, "If you don't want to marry me, would you introduce me to your friend Anne?" I knew then that I should not let this wonderful man slip away.

"If we get married, we'll go abroad every five years," he promised. This was a time when few people went to Europe even once. I did not realize that he was talking about the congresses where he expected to give papers. As it turned out, we traveled much more often than his conservative estimate.

We became engaged on April 17, and our wedding was June 17. My mother arranged for the First Baptist Church in St. Joseph (where I grew up) and did all the work, including handwritten invitations. Mother's Day came in between, and a simple card Charles sent my mother without my knowledge won her heart. She always loved her son-in-law. After wishing for a son, she had given up. I finally gave her a worthy one.

My father was opposed to the marriage because a research career would be less lucrative than a practice. He threatened to cut off support for my final year of medical school, but my father-in-law-to-be, knowing his son needed an intelligent, well-educated wife, offered to borrow against his pension. He didn't need to because, in time, my father came around.

I found a beautiful Swiss organdy cocktail-length dress, and borrowed my Aunt Bide's sapphire necklace. I wanted none of the trappings of female submissiveness, such as a veil or being given away like chattel from one man (father) to another (husband-to-be). Charles's nine-year-old nephew, Bobby, served as acolyte and lighted candles at twilight, and Charles's sister-in-law, John's wife, Gloria, a professional contralto, sang *Some Enchanted Evening* from *South Pacific.* During the music, Charles walked across the church and escorted me to the altar for the ceremony. We recited the vows we'd written. I have never seen a wedding more beautiful.

Because of the seventeens involved, Charles considered the seventeenth of each month our "monthiversary" and gave me a red rose each time it came around. He had explained that Russians (not the communists) are romantic.

Charles's idea had been to take, again, a summer job at the Center for Communicable Diseases in Atlanta, but I wanted my first taste of Europe. He acknowledged the validity of my argument that this was our last summer-long vacation, so he cashed in his war bonds and we planned our summer abroad.

In an age when Americans feared the Russians (even those of Russian parentage), Charles had passport problems. Mine came in good time, but his was delayed. A lawyer friend advised him to write to explain he was not and had never been a Communist. I couldn't understand how, if they wanted to think he was a spy, that would persuade them otherwise. After Charles minored in history and was a champion debater in college, the FBI had offered him a job. It amused me to think of this honest, straightforward man as a spy. Nonetheless, the lawyer's strategy apparently worked, because Charles's passport arrived on our wedding day.

We headed to New York to board a Norwegian ship that our interns and medical students group had chartered, but the Coast Guard had declared it unsafe for having too few fire extinguishers. Charles and I were interviewed on television about the hundreds of students in New York waiting for a ship. (We were fortunate to be staying with the Bouquets, thus saving travel money.) To meet our need, President Harry Truman made the S.S. *Ballou* available, an army transport ship going over empty to bring home military personnel. The ship had been used for trials of Dramamine for motion sickness because she rolled and pitched and yawed worse than any other. Charles was seasick on the crossing but happy to be married. As the ship ploughed on to Rotterdam, I took Dutch lessons onboard. The teacher praised my accent, which we attributed to my having heard all four grandparents speak Dutch on occasion. When I asked my grandfather to teach me Dutch, he was too intimidated to take on the esteemed role of teacher.

The first name on the passenger manifest was that of my high school debate partner and the salutatorian, Art Ablin, who had gone to a different medical school. Charles and Art struck up a lifelong friendship. We traveled around Holland together, the boys ate smoked eel on the streets, and Art headed off to Spain while Charles and I went to Paris to celebrate Bastille Day, July 14. Over the years we would see Art at my high school reunions, where the class considered Charles a kind of class in-law.

At reunions I noticed that Art made a point of greeting all his classmates, not just his friends. Later, when he and Charles and I got together, he commented that nobody seemed to have any special interests. When he would ask what they were doing, they would reply, "Why, nothing. I'm retired." This was in contrast to Art, who like most physicians is still working beyond the age of sixty-five. He is now reviewing grant proposals at UCSF (University of California at San Francisco) Medical School. When he and his wife travel, he collects fern seeds to grow a collection back home, while his wife goes birding.

At a later reunion Art told Charles about his painful hip, which made walking very hard. As a pediatrician at UCSF, he had had access to specialists, but none had helped. Charles had a waiter bring a telephone book and told Art to stand on it with one foot. Magically, the pain vanished. Charles explained that no specialist had observed that Art's legs were of unequal length. With a lift on the short side, he could walk comfortably. Since then, whenever we meet or talk on the phone, Art always remembers this incident with appreciation. And I remember it with pride in my husband.

✳

Europe was absolutely flat from the fighting during the war, and we saw nine countries in nine weeks on $5 a day. We stayed in student dormitories with cold showers, rode to Vienna with friends in their rented car, and visited many churches and museums. I loved being called *"Madame."* Charles showed me places he had worked or visited in the Occupation, such as the concentration camp at Dachau, which he had seen before the ashes were cleaned out of the ovens and the sign had been removed that read in German: WASH YOUR HANDS AFTER WORK. CLEANLINESS IS YOUR DUTY.

We stayed in the Salzburg Schloss and went to the festival, where we heard soprano Elisabeth Schwarzkopf sing in Beethoven's opera *Fidelio.* The year being 1950, an even decade, Oberammergau had reinstituted its centuries-old Passion play, which I had learned about from my German tutor, and I had secured tickets before we left home. Charles and I laughed over how whenever I would say, "I want to go to (fill in the blank)," Charles would get us there. He took me to one of his favorite spots for R&R, Lugano, a tranquil Alpine town and lake where they celebrated Swiss Independence Day on

August 1 with beautiful fireworks. I was learning how to travel from an expert. We stayed at the Hotel Terminus in each city to be in the center of activity, for easy arrival and departure on trains. We started collecting small countries, in this case Liechtenstein. I wrote postcards to thank people for wedding gifts. Charles joked that I ate my weight in Wiener schnitzel.

By fall we headed back home for my mother's delicious vegetable soup and our last year of medical school.

The final year of medical school rushed past. Charles had acute appendicitis but in three days was carrying groceries home to our apartment. We each had a free quarter, and Charles used his to complete his research at the School of Public Health. I spent mine at the University of Chicago and stayed with the couple I called my parents-in-law-in-law, Charles's brother's wife's parents, the Sandalises, who lived nearby. In addition to clinical studies and applications for internships, we had not only finals to prepare for but also boards. We were advised to take state, not national, boards. We took those examinations right after finals, but had to review our basic sciences from two and more years back. I dreamed of someday enjoying the month of May without the pressure of exams.

My parents and Aunt Bide came to Baltimore for the graduation, and Charles and I packed the Studebaker, said good-bye to Iza, and headed west to Chicago.

Three friends graduate.

CHAPTER 5

RHEUMATOLOGY RESEARCHER AND CLINICIAN (1951–1956)

BOTH OF US HAD BEEN accepted for internships at the University of Illinois Research and Education Hospital in Chicago. It was a relief to pack everything we owned into Charles's Studebaker and head west. Since they had no rooming arrangements for married interns, we shared Charles's room, and I don't know how it held two people's clothes and uniforms. Intern's salary was $15 per month plus room and board. For the next few years after our internship, we rented an apartment above a little chapel from Dick Young, the Anglican priest for the medical center. Our main expenses were for keeping the Studebaker running and occasional concert tickets.

While we were in Chicago, many people helped us as we got our professional lives organized. Although Charles's brother John and his wife and children had moved to Seattle, Gloria's parents, the Sandalises, were kind and helpful to us. Sam (Seraphim) had emigrated from Greece but continued to support his mother and four sisters. He had married Fanchon, the daughter of a farm family. She was a splendid cook, and the two of them ran a mom and pop restaurant in downtown Chicago for many years. They also often had us over for Sunday dinner, and I can still remember her delicious stewed chicken. Fanchon would run our laundry in her washer and dryer while I fell asleep on the couch after a hard week. I smile when I remember how one day Sam happened to mention that sometimes he became "paralyzed." Alarmed, we immediately made appropriate inquiries. "Sometimes after dinner I just can't keep my eyes open," he explained. This reinforced our teaching that physicians have to be alert to the possibility that patients are misusing words that we consider in our domain.

One advantage of Chicago was that it was just ninety miles from my parents' home north of Benton Harbor, Michigan. When we could get the same weekend off, we would go there and have my mother feed and rest us for the difficult upcoming week. In St. Joseph, the twin city of Benton Harbor, at that time a popular getaway spot for Chicagoans was the Whitcomb Hotel. They featured comedians trying out their acts before taking them on the Borscht Belt circuit in the Poconos. Those Jewish comedians were very funny, on the order of Sid Caesar, whom we heard on television in the staff lounge when we were on call on Saturday nights. I also liked a drink that the Whitcomb offered, a "pink squirrel" with grenadine and nut flavoring. Charles loved to dance even though he couldn't identify the beat, and I would have to whisper it into his ear.

Both of us had been neglecting our teeth while in medical school. An allergist Charles met recommended Bernard Rappaport, D.D.S., his uncle. This hardworking perfectionist considered it his mission to take top-of-the-line dentistry to people of moderate means, which we certainly were on our salaries in training. Bernard's work was so beautiful and flawless that dentists states away could recognize it by looking into one's mouth. He took out all our old crumbling fillings and replaced them with gold. We had his first appointment at seven in the morning, and then went on to work. Bernard also toyed with an invention, a device with rods to pierce a roast to conduct heat into it and thereby cook the meat more evenly. He invited favorite patients out on Sundays to test the results. We kept returning to Chicago for dental updates as long as he was able to practice. (I went in August each year, so as to shop in Marshall Field's for Christmas toys and games for our boys.)

Charles's surgery rotation produced Siamese twins. Unlike those joined at the hip, who were often left to live together that way, these were joined at the head, involving their brains, and there was no way for one twin to carry the other around, so separation, while hazardous, was the only option. The surgical residents were excited about this rare opportunity. Charles, with his distaste for surgery, was happy to give a resident the opportunity to take his place as an intern, to scrub on this case, which involved holding retractors for six or eight hours. The twin more at risk died. (Only recently has pediatric neurosurgeon Ben Carson, M.D. successfully separated two such twins with both surviving.)

A much more interesting case for a biochemist/internist showed up when Charles rotated for several weeks at Cook County Hospital, then the largest general hospital anywhere, just across the street from our Research and Education Hospital. A homeless man on an atrocious diet had acquired scurvy! Nobody had seen a case for many years because everyone knew that it was prevented by the vitamin C in a normal diet. What Charles learned from this case surfaced twenty years later and led to a fascinating sideline in his career, as I shall describe later.

Our internship gave us a two-week vacation, and so we

camped out to the Southwest to see Mesa Verde. It happened to coincide with the McCarthy hearings, which we listened to for hours on the car radio. Congressman Joseph McCarthy said that Communists had infiltrated the government as well as the entertainment industry. Fifty years later the Venona decrypts were declassified, confirming McCarthy's charges. The popular write-up was in *Harper's Magazine*.

After internship I was undecided what career to follow or what to do next. I spent a year in pathology and then worked as a pediatrician for the City of Chicago, in a cancer prevention clinic, and in radiation research at the Fermi Lab of the University of Chicago, while still floundering about my future.

By the end of our required internship, Charles, almost thirty-six, was ready to pursue a straight course to become a rheumatologist. This necessitated a residency in internal medicine, which he took at the University of Chicago. He not only became head resident there but also met and worked with Charlie Huggins, urologist and Nobel Prize laureate, and with Alan Kenyon, endocrinologist. He also met Del Bergenstahl, a friend of Charles's brother John. Del had access to radioisotopes newly available from work on "the bomb," by then valuable in certain kinds of medical research. Del taught Charles how to use radioactive sulfur to study cartilage metabolism in rats. In this way the early part of Charles's rheumatology research was launched. Tragically, Del died very young. Charles always said that if Del had lived, he would have won the Nobel Prize.

It may have been the luck of the draw, or perhaps the admissions personnel sent high-profile patients to the services where Charles was low man, but he always seemed to be getting admissions that were interesting either medically or as celebrities. While still at Hopkins, Charles examined Carlos Julio Arosemena, a colorful politician and onetime president of Ecuador, deposed in a military coup and exiled to Panama. Arosemena came to Hopkins for a different medical problem but was also in an early stage of Hansen's disease, the euphemism for leprosy. Besides the usual reasons of patient privacy and for Arosemena's possible future in politics, the disease had to be kept quiet not to start panic.

While a resident in the Department of Medicine, as a biochemist, Charles prided himself that, while he could not save all his patients (no physician could), no patient of his ever died in electrolyte (chemical) imbalance.

In the course of their rheumatology research with patients, Charles visited the Joliet Correctional Center, a maximum-security prison outside of Chicago in Crest Hill, to draw blood from inmate volunteers for use as normal controls. There Charles met an inmate, Nathan Leopold, of the notorious Leopold and Loeb duo who had killed a fourteen-year-old boy for thrills. Leopold was thought to be the passive follower in the crime. The two had been defended by the illustrious Clarence Darrow, who got them life imprisonment, his brilliant argument against the death penalty saving them from execution. Richard Loeb died young while in prison. Leopold spent most of his life working in the prison laboratory. He assisted Charles in his collection of blood. Years later, in his sixties, Loeb was freed despite having been sentenced "without parole," and emigrated to the Caribbean.

Charles was resident on the service where physicist Enrico Fermi came in for treatment of stomach cancer. Having come to regret his role in the development of the atomic bomb, this Nobel Prize winner gave up the struggle to live. Charles comforted his grieving widow, Laura Fermi.

A more joyful patient on Charles's service was the gospel singer Mahalia Jackson. In appreciation for the care she received she put on a special concert for the medical personnel. The audience kept calling her back for encores, until the only way she had to signal the end was to march out singing her signature hymn *When the Saints Go Marching In*. She went on to be involved in the civil rights movement and sang in Washington, D.C., right before Dr. Martin Luther King Jr. gave his "I Have a Dream" speech.

The chancellor of the university was admitted for his annual checkup, and the senior staff members were embarrassed to do the customary rectal examination. Charles performed the exam, saying the chancellor deserved the same good care given to everyone else, including the homeless treated in the clinic. (In those days the best medical care available was on charity wards in university hospitals.) Members of the wives' club and their spouses met once at the chancellor's house. After a potluck supper, we all went to play with the chancellor's miniature train set, which took up the entire attic.

While in Chicago Charles received a letter from the Walter Reed Army Medical Library (now Walter Reed Army Medical Center) in Bethesda, Maryland, requesting a portrait. It was to be in a collection of 400 of those who had made the most important contributions to medicine, going back to the Renaissance. We assume it was for his work on army rations in healthy volunteers because his serious research in rheumatology was just beginning and was not yet in print. This called for the finest photographer available, so I made inquiries and learned that in Chicago that was the Bachrach Studios. Charles had two portraits taken, one in a white coat for Walter Reed (seen on the cover of this book), the other in a business suit for relatives.

By the mid-1950s, the medical community recognized nutrition as a specialty, and Charles was grandfathered into the newly formed American Board of Nutrition as a diplomate. (This too was based on his army work.)

⁂

One vacation we took during those Chicago years was by air through the large islands of the Caribbean, with stopovers as long as we wished at every stop. My parents went along with us, but my mother disliked heat and tropics and said that was the only time Miami looked good.

As Charles wrote:

> We visited the Caribbean. Of all the independent countries, territories, and dependencies, we found Haiti the most backward, and, unfortunately, the most poverty-stricken and dictator-driven. One morning we walked from our little hotel, along open gutters flowing with sewage, to the downtown, looking for sights, souvenirs, and local activity. The harbor area was the poorest we had ever seen, with shacks built on mounds of rubbish and coconut husks, and constructed of cardboard boxes and flattened gallon tins.
>
> The center of activity was an open market called the Fer Merchand, from its support structure composed of iron filigree. Local shoppers dressed in bright skirts and blouses of primary colors walked along booths that offered kitchen and household items, piles of shoes, dresses and infants' wear, tropical fruits and vegetables, meats crawling with flies, and fish from the ocean.
>
> We were drawn to woodcarvings for mementoes of the trip. After pricing the goods at several booths (nothing carried a price tag), we found carved heads

with hair in the style from colonial days and entered into negotiations with the saleslady. I made bids and counter-bids in simple French, and bought two. The booth owner gave us a carved fish as a sign that I was a gentleman she liked doing business with.

Back at the hotel, we showed our finds to fellow travelers, one of whom asked to be taken to the booth the next day. On arrival we were disappointed to find the booth closed, curtain pulled down, not a sign of commercial activity. I asked her friend in the adjoining booth when the lady would be back.

"Ah, m'sieu, you have not heard. Madame had such a good day yesterday—she even gave a fish to the customer for good luck—and took today off for holiday."

Another vacation from our Chicago years we took through New England, including Acadia National Park in Maine, through New Brunswick to Nova Scotia and on to Newfoundland, then by small boat to Saint Pierre, of Saint-Pierre and Miquelon, the only vestige of the French empire in North America. When I studied the French and Indian Wars, they explained that part of the treaty as "fishing islands in the Grand Banks." Where we stayed, Madame cooked wonderful French food for us for $5 a day. We visited the hospital and heard about tuberculosis up there, before good antibiotics for the Koch bacillus. Finally we boarded a ship that served Labrador carrying passengers, freight, and mail. At each stop the ship's doctor (a second-year medical student) went ashore to do rounds. We went with him to help and saw a postpartum case and a cut by an *ulu* (a sharp instrument for trimming hides). Our ship went as far north as possible until stopped by the drifting pack ice.

We and another couple ate at the captain's table. Norton took a picture of every iceberg we passed. Charles took a picture of every Eskimo (they were flattered). I took pictures of puffins.

Unhappy over my stalled career and worried that having become a physician had been a mistake, I went into psychoanalysis with Dr. Helen Beiser. Freudian psychoanalysis was at the peak of its popularity in the mid-twentieth century. As my work with Dr. Beiser progressed, I became interested in psychiatry. She concurred with my choice of specialty. That decision was my major accomplishment in Chicago. I have never regretted it.

We suffered one large setback in Chicago. We were excited about our first pregnancy, and I decided, since we had been led to believe that pregnancy is so natural and normal, what fun it would be to be attended by my friend who had just finished her residency in obstetrics. But I had no sooner gone to visit Iza in New York and shopped at Klein's and Ohrbach's for kangaroo skirts and pretty tops than trouble started. Not only was mine not a normal pregnancy but my friend was not firmly enough grounded in obstetrics to recognize the trouble. It was not until she called in her mentor from Northwestern University that the problem was diagnosed. The pregnancy could not have been saved by more timely recognition, but I could have been spared pain and anguish. I resolved in the future always to consult the ranking specialist for any medical problem.

The time had come for Charles to get an academic appointment.

Charles Denko at forty.

Charles W. Denko, Ph.D., M.D.
Portrait requested by Army Medical Museum.

CHAPTER 6

CHARLES BECOMES A PROFESSOR
(1956–1960)

HAVING COMPLETED HIS INTERNAL MEDICINE residency at Chicago, Charles was finally ready to devote himself to the subspecialty he had set his sights on fifteen years earlier. He accepted a position as Instructor (later Assistant Professor) in the Rheumatology Division of the University of Michigan College of Medicine. Thus he established his place in that new specialty to which hundreds of thousands of patients, including children, were turning for help.

Rheumatology is that branch of medicine concerned with the body's connective tissues, joints and cartilage, and the "stroma" or connective tissue cells that hold together the various cells that are doing the body's work. Rheumatology includes over a hundred kinds of arthritis, lupus, and other autoimmune diseases. (Charles once told me that he had seen all but one of these, a variety that occurs only in some remote part of the world.) He wanted to find out how changes in the body's chemistry cause rheumatologic diseases and how those diseases alter the biochemistry of the body. With this information, treatment beyond simple pain relief becomes possible, just as he had hoped since his days at Penn State as a student of A. K. Anderson. Charles knew the importance of his research. He was establishing his place in the new specialty of rheumatology.

At the same time I was accepted as a psychiatry resident at the University of Michigan.

The timing of our move was perfect. My cousin Eunice Noordyk Lampkin's husband, Chad, had just received his M.D. from the University of Michigan. They had built a house on Huron River Drive at Dexter, and, with Chad preparing to go on to his residency, they needed to sell it. It fitted our need and we bought it. Therefore we began each day with a pleasant twenty-minute drive into Ann Arbor along the river, where we often saw great blue herons standing in the shallows. In Dexter we were still close enough to Benton Harbor for an occasional weekend of rest and relaxation with my parents.

Charles was beginning to treat and study rheumatology patients in Michigan's specialty clinic, and to collect data about their biochemical deviances from normal, but for several years he was still writing and publishing his findings, with colleagues, from his days at Chicago.

As an academic, Charles's out-of-town meetings were beginning, at which he presented papers and we sightsaw the area. When he was scheduled to give a paper at a congress in San Francisco, we headed out via the Grand Canyon, the first time for both of us. From my Aunt Bide I had learned about the mule-train trip by Bright Angel Trail down the canyon wall to the Colorado River. Charles encouraged me to take it. He explained to me that with his weak left leg he could not mount a saddle animal, since the animals had been trained not to accept a rider from the right, but he never wanted anyone to miss an opportunity because of his disability. Arriving just the day before, I was lucky to get the thirtieth mule of three trains of ten, and so I had that marvelous trip down thousands of feet of sedimentation representing millions of years of mountain growth. That day Charles stayed in the campground and put the finishing touches on his paper for the meeting.

At that time the higher level of Lake Mead would soon flood the beautiful Rainbow Bridge in the National Monument in Utah. Again, Charles encouraged me to go, and he waited while two women friends and I packed in to see the bridge and the desert sky strewn with what appeared to be millions of stars. I took a photograph of our guide, mounted, contemplating canyons vanishing to the horizon. When I got home I sold one-time rights to that photo for $250, an excellent price for that time, to a pharmaceutical company that was sending a series of postcards to every physician, advertising a medication for gastric hyperacidity. Each card showed a single figure in a vacation spot, with the caption "Nothing will help your ulcer patient like a vacation, except (name of the medication)."

Charles gave another paper at the Pan American Congress held in Toronto. We used that as a launching pad for a camping trip out to western Canada, to Banff and Lake Louise. When we learned of an excursion by caterpillar tractor up onto the Athabasca Glacier, we hastened to get tickets. We could see whirlpools of meltwater dropping down through cracks in the blue glacier on their way out to its base. Our naturalist guide drew our attention to the amount of recession of the glacier since it was first measured early in the twentieth century.

One goal on that trip had been to spend a luxurious, romantic night in the world famous Chateau Lake Louise, at the cost, then, of $60. But we saw Cowichan (Native American) sweaters, knitted from the natural colors of sheep's wool, at $30 each, so we bought two and wore them all our lives. We were content to walk through the hotel.

Our time in Michigan was saddened by two more pregnancy failures, a stillborn girl and a boy too premature to survive and buried in Ann Arbor. By then the obstetrician knew the problem, and we had a plan for how to try again.

It was soon apparent that Charles's career path was blocked at Michigan, and he decided to look elsewhere. When Ohio State University offered him a position as Assistant Professor of Medicine, with his own lab for animal research, he began arranging for us to move to the Columbus, Ohio, area, and my mother came to Dexter to help me recover from the death of our newborn son. Knowing that I needed country and water, and, like his father, trying to please his wife, Charles found a house that I would be living in to this day if that had been possible. At the end of Watt Road, built into and hidden behind a hill, was a pinkish-gray stone house, on three acres, with a huge sycamore, a small horse stable, and a dammed stream making a pond for ice skating.

Having completed only two years of the three required for my specialty of psychiatry, I arranged to transfer to the psychiatry department at Ohio State for my final year. By the time I reached Gahanna, Charles was already working in his lab and the rheumatology clinic. I soon started my third year of psychiatry residency.

Not long after our move, I was pregnant again. As planned, I postponed my remaining months of residency and went on "bed rest," meaning being horizontal, lying on the couch, and hiring a housekeeper/caretaker, the strategy that was felt necessary if I were to carry a baby to term. Charles helped at home and brought papers to work on at home on evenings and weekends. I also worked on papers on my clipboard. Even reading became tiresome, although I enjoyed, among others, a four-volume history of mathematics. It was a monotonous and worrisome eight months. We had decided that if this pregnancy were unsuccessful, it would be our last.

One hot Sunday afternoon in August, friends came to visit, followed by an adorable half-grown black-and-white spaniel puppy. I asked whether we should give their dog a dish of water.

"*Our* dog?" We thought she was *your* dog. She followed us in."

Cleo became our first dog. She could open doors with doorknobs.

❋

Over my mask I watched my obstetrician's eyes over his mask as he tested the level of anesthesia on my abdomen and proceeded to lay me open for the section. Then he showed me the baby and said, "You've got a keeper this time, a perfect baby boy," and nodded to the anesthesiologist to put me to sleep for the closure.

Our eldest surviving child, Christopher, was born December 20, 1960. Walking down an unplowed driveway, we carried home this perfect newborn wrapped in the carriage robe given by a patient I had treated in Illinois. When we put Christopher into his crib, Cleo saw her duty and responsibility and positioned herself underneath.

More than any other event—single or married, this school or that, one or another career, North America or a different continent—having a child changes your life forever.

*"What I learn from patients I take to the lab, and what
I learn in the lab I take back to help patients."*
— Charles W. Denko Ph.D., M.D.
I called this "Chuck's tango."

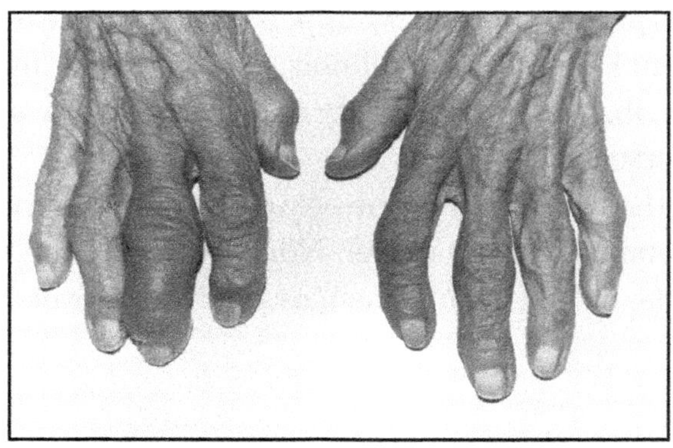

Severe arthritis in elderly woman.

CHAPTER 7

CHARLES'S LIFE AS A PROFESSOR AND FATHER (1960–1968)

OUR LIFE AS A two-generation family began with Christopher's birth.

My mother came to help us get started. Her visit was one of many, always timed to help us, later by staying with the children when we traveled. We kept Mrs. Bokros to care for Christopher when I returned to the hospital to finish my residency. To give him the advantage of maternal antibodies, I breast-fed him and pumped the milk at the hospital for the next day.

During this time Charles continued his ^{35}S studies, treated patients in the rheumatology clinic, and taught students and residents, both by lecturing and by going on "rounds" and demonstrating the signs shown by the patients they were treating.

Before completing my residency, I had converted our long, old-fashioned porch to a small office and waiting room where I began seeing a few patients in the evening while Charles cared for Christopher.

Many dogs were abandoned at our dead end, and we found homes for those we could not keep and in some cases their puppies. Small, all-black Sybil and border-collie mix White-foot completed the canine part of our family.

⁂

Soon after I was back at work, I happened to be assigned Jean Anderson, a patient who had made a suicidal gesture because of being overwhelmed by three children under five years of age. Working with her, I learned that the best time of her life had been when she worked as an executive secretary at the Ohio legislature (until the other party won an election). When she was discharged, I kept her as a patient. I also sent her to Charles, who was in need of secretarial help. Jean became his gold standard, the best he ever had. He also gave her time to me when I needed help in getting papers ready for publication. She and I remained friends even after we had to leave the Columbus area, and when she died, young, of breast cancer, I gave the eulogy.

I was assigned a patient, a fifty-year-old woman with severe depression and convulsive seizures, who sat immobile and was mute. I found her to have tetanic spasms and traced the cause to a rare endocrinologic problem. I was able to write up her case and a hundred others we found in the world literature, as a freestanding supplement, hence a book, and also as my dissertation for my master's degree from Michigan.

⁂

During my eight months on the couch gently easing my pregnancy with Christopher to term, Charles, who did everything he could think of to make my life easier and more pleasant, came in one day waving a *Columbus Sunday Dispatch,* saying,

"Here's something that might interest you."

He gave me an article about the then-new organization for people with an IQ in the upper 2 percent, originating in England, the Mensa Society. "Look," I pointed out to him, "it says that members are willing to be subjects for 'qualified researchers.' Hey, that's me! By their IQ requirement they have gathered a study population with that one unifying trait (or close to one; they also share the wish to belong, whereas many who qualify do not join). I could do a study on highly intelligent adults no longer of interest to the educational system. Another thing— as members we could meet interesting people in lines of work other than medical."

As I considered how to proceed, with my ever-handy clipboard, I decided that we should join first, which would have to wait until after the pregnancy. Then, once I was mobile with Christopher safely delivered, we sent off for our scores. Charles was lucky—one of his schools supplied his, but two of my schools couldn't or wouldn't, so I had to take the intelligence test Mensa offers, the Cattell, which is not used much in this country.

After we were both members, I prepared a questionnaire of twenty-five open-ended questions, which I mailed to the Columbus chapter members, and, after our move to Cuyahoga, to the Northeast Ohio members. I analyzed all answers from the 159 responders and wrote a chapter on their answers to each question. The book is *Through the Keyhole at Gifted Men and Women.*

We used Mensa as a social outlet, attending not only regular meetings but also parties and picnics in Old Man's Cave, a state park in the foothills of Appalachia in Southeast Ohio. (Old Man's Cave is not a real cave, but an overhanging ledge.)

⁂

During this period we joined a welcoming church, Gahanna Community Church, where all the boys were baptized.

The Christmas when Christopher was one, Charles made him a huge snowman. I photographed him in his sky-blue snowsuit, looking up into the snowman's face with awe. That photo gave me an idea for the following year: to name the picture "First Christmas" (although it was Christopher's second, since he was born on December 20), mount it on purple construction paper, and have Charles, whose printing was beautiful, letter the title and our signature. We sent these out as our Christmas card.

As long as we had children in elementary school, each year I took a Christmas- or winter-themed photo of one or more of the three, to use the following year. I often had the child or children looking away from the camera so as to represent not our children but *"Jederkind."* Charles contributed his beautiful printing.

⁂

Charles was continuing his work with his ^{35}S studies on rat cartilage. When the European Congress of Rheumatology called for papers for their meeting in Rome in 1963, he submitted one on that material and, as usual, was accepted. My mother came to take care of Christopher, and Charles and I boarded a ship for Italy.

After Charles's presentation, a representative from the Swiss pharmaceutical firm Robapharm sought him out. He described their product Rumalon, a water extract of ground bone and cartilage from slaughterhouses, administered only by injection, and used all over Europe for rheumatologic complaints.

One question had been whether the reported improvement in patients had been a placebo effect. He asked whether Charles would be interested in studying Rumalon in rats. Charles agreed and said, "My controls won't have a placebo effect. I'll give the controls a sham injection." (This was a standard method in controlled experiments, to give the controls the vehicle without the ingredient that is being tested.)

After all the import red tape, the Rumalon had arrived, and Charles's experiments showed that it had a positive biologic effect on rats' cartilage. Robapharm was so delighted that they offered to send us to the Pan American Congress in Santiago, Chile, later that year to present his findings. At that time we flew separately in case of an accident that would make Christopher an orphan, and I left several days early to detour to Machu Picchu. After the meeting Robapharm paid for us to spend a week in the Lake District of Chile, farther south, with its smoking volcanoes. Robapharm credited Charles's talk with the sale of thousands of dollars' worth of Rumalon in South America and worldwide. In 1963 that was a lot of Rumalon.

Subsequently Charles was authorized to use Rumalon in a patient trial. About 20 percent of his patients with osteoarthritis of the hip not only improved but even showed regrowth of cartilage! (This had never before been observed.) This eliminated or at least delayed the need for surgery. He had one patient with a flair for the dramatic. The wife of an antique car aficionado, she and her husband attended their annual convention with her, as usual, in a wheelchair. To her friends' astonishment, when the band struck up, she got out of her wheelchair and proceeded to the dance floor to dance. She always liked it when Charles took her films to show at meetings. Often when he would put them up, viewers would comment that he had them up wrong, and he would have to point out the dates burned into the films at time of exposure. No one before had ever demonstrated regrowth of cartilage.

So why is Rumalon not in the formulary now? Because at that time our FDA (Federal Drug Administration) had introduced a new requirement that all medications had to be synthesized. This eliminated other medications such as the desiccated thyroid I had taken for years, as well as Rumalon. (We shall see later what became of Rumalon worldwide thirty years later.)

⁎

The following year, when Christopher was three, found me pregnant again. It was a shaky pregnancy from the start and did not seem to be settling down, although I was taking the only treatment then available for a troubled pregnancy, intramuscular progesterone. We knew that we were taking a risk. If the embryo survived and was a girl, she might have a bad side effect known as adrenogenital syndrome.

The problem was that Charles had submitted a paper for a meeting in Aix-les-Bains, France, and we had booked passage to Gibraltar. We had to make a decision about this pregnancy with such a dismal outlook. Finally, as my bleeding worsened, we decided that the pregnancy was doomed anyway and would not last more than a couple days, a week at the most, and we might as well leave for Europe. We took the Twentieth Century Limited to New York, and I fell asleep to the gentle clackety-clack on the rail bed. By morning my bleeding had slacked off a little. We boarded ship and I went back to bed, and the outlook seemed more hopeful. After a couple days it looked as though the progesterone was doing its work and the pregnancy had finally stabilized. I began to move around the ship. One evening the captain invited me to dance, but I explained about my problem and declined. We had a day in Madeira, where they ride sleds with wooden runners down hills with cobbled streets, but of course I passed that up. We made it to Aix-les-Bains without incident, and I attended the only fashion show of my life, for the wives at the meeting. With minimal travel we made it back home with the pregnancy intact and growing, and again I went on "bed rest" for the remaining six months.

I had gained a little confidence, and this time I saw a few patients. What was different was that I put the patient at my desk and me on my couch. That was when a patient came to me who was so afraid that he would be discharged if the armed forces found out about his condition that he gave me the wrong branch of service (what did I know about the uniforms?) and a fake name, and always paid in cash. But I got him through his problem, to the satisfaction of both of us. Charles suggested that I take good notes and write him up, which I did.

The day Christopher was four years old, I went to the hospital for my section, and we were rewarded on the winter solstice, December 21, 1964, with little Nicholas. At one of the many hospital parties, a friend asked Charles what we had had, then told him, "I have a boy and a girl, myself."

"Well, you don't always get the set," was Charles's rejoinder.

Our final reward for patience came nineteen months later, when our final child, Timothey, was born on July 28, 1966. He was named for his father, being given the middle name of Charles, like the other two.

Many of our colleagues unwind by spending a day on the links. After we settled into a routine, I asked Charles whether he intended to join a country club to play golf with other docs, as a way to relax and get a little exercise, since he could easily make it around the course and was a pretty good duffer.

"No, I'd rather take up gardening, like my father. The bottomland soil near the horse stable is good, and the boys can help me. (You can imagine how much help they were.) Even if each tomato costs $3.78, it'll be exercise for me, without fees, and I'll be right at home." He produced some tomatoes and green peppers, and we joked about how the tomatoes cost $3.42 each. One year he put in pumpkins with the intention of having homegrown jack-o-lanterns.

My mother, who always loved Charles, decided to make him a pumpkin pie out of his own pumpkins, but they were so tough to cut up that she practically wore calluses on her hands. She said she wouldn't undertake it again. Charles appreciated the pie for what it was, a sign of her affection for the son she always wanted. The pumpkins were also too tough to carve for jack-o-lanterns.

While at OSU, Charles was offered lifetime support at whatever institution would give him laboratory facilities and office space. However, while this was in negotiations, the offer was withdrawn. While I was not following the ins and outs, what I believe happened was this: Geigy Pharmaceuticals had medications for arthritis. Geigy's representative in our area was very interested in Charles's work and sent him to give talks to various groups. I believe this man was working on the lifetime support idea, but then Geigy was sold to another company. While this lifetime support sounded like a good idea, it could have created problems if it had gone through.

We lived in our rural paradise on Watt Road long enough for Christopher to complete second grade. He brought home a flyer about a Y-sponsored organization for fathers and sons, called Indian Guides. He and Charles joined, Christopher as Red Cloud. I jokingly called Charles "Big Chief Thunder Cloud" because he was so good-natured. They did many interesting things, such as visiting Indian mounds; they brought home flint from Flint Ridge, where Native Americans had agreed to suspend hostilities because all the tribes needed flint for arrowheads. Indian Guides even tried to teach the amenities, including sending out invitations to the meetings held in members' homes.

❉

When Christopher was seven and in second grade, the Pan American Congress was held in Mexico City. I thought it would be a good first trip outside the country for him, and I was proud of how well he did. In fact other wives said they wished they had thought to bring children. He went with us on the wives' trip to the Pyramids of the Sun and of the Moon outside Mexico City. (I was delighted when, years later, we took Christopher by ship to the Sea of Cortez to see a solar eclipse, that he recognized an unlabeled photograph of the Sun Pyramid decorating the hall.) At the banquet he saw the Ballet Foklorico. (Back home he printed "menus" for the Indian Guides meeting in our house: Kool-Aid, cookies, at each place, just like at the banquet.) After the meeting we took a bus to the Yucatan to see Chichen Itza and Uxmal. I thought I had made a mistake to bring him, until he got safely back down those steep steps without handrails.

❉

Charles's career path was blocked again, by a man younger than himself and just above him at OSU. (This was because of the years Charles spent on his Ph.D. and in the army.) He was offered a position as director of research in the Scott Research Laboratory at Fairview General Hospital in Cleveland, with time in the Division of Rheumatology at Case Western Reserve

University and a day a week for private practice. This would give him time for what I came to call his "tango" back and forth between patients and laboratory. What he encountered in patients he studied in the lab. What he learned in the lab he used to help patients.

He accepted this offer and spent the spring of 1968 commuting a day a week the 125 miles, to start setting up the lab, ordering supplies, hiring a lab technician and a secretary, and looking for a house for us. When he showed me 21160 Avalon Drive in Rocky River, on a cliff overlooking Lake Erie, I knew it would have to replace our lost country living. Charles's humor about buying it consisted of "going to the bank to play Monopoly with the banker," i.e., taking stock certificates out of our box and putting them into the bank's.

I hated to leave Watt Road. I loved those three acres with running stream and pond, our huge sycamore, and beautiful pinkish-gray stone house built into the hillside. If I could have, I would have moved it stone by stone.

But, like others before us, we were driven out of Eden.

Four Denko boys playing horsie.
"The boys want some ice cream."

—Charles, knowing I'm trying to keep his weight down.

Platypus.
Egg-laying mammal with a poison gland.

CHAPTER 8

THE DENKO FAMILY IN ROCKY RIVER, OHIO, AND CANBERRA, AUSTRALIA (1968–1976)

MOVING THREE BOYS, three dogs, and more books than the movers had ever before transported caused me to tell Betty Bucher, our helpful new neighbor, "I hope you like us, because the next time I move it's going to be feet first." On Timothey's birthday when he was two, July 28, we ate his cake in a family room looking out over Lake Erie, with unopened boxes piled to the ceiling.

I found a mother's helper who was about to start college in the fall, who kept the children safe while I settled us.

In 1969 Geneva College honored Charles with its Distinguished Service Award. Over the years he often returned to Geneva, sometimes giving a talk to the chemistry students, and we both gave talks to the premeds.

Because of his advance preparations Charles was able to move right ahead with his research while gradually building up his patient clientele. In time he took on membership on committees relating to medicine, sometimes dealing with his special knowledge about rheumatology. One such was the Medical Advisory Committee for the Lupus Foundation. He also served on the committee dealing with the problem of "orphan drugs," medications for diseases so rare that there are not enough patients with the disease to make it profitable for a pharmaceutical company to market the drug they need. The committees usually met at the National Institutes of Health in Bethesda, Maryland.

These trips offered an opportunity for Charles to get back in touch with his old friend from Ellwood City, Andy Tkach, White House physician to President Nixon. Andy offered Charles a job as his assistant, but Andy's wife advised against it: "It's great for Andy but terrible for the family. We hardly ever see him." Charles declined because he wished to continue his tango between observing and treating patients with rheumatologic disorders and taking what he learned from them to the lab to study the biochemistry of connective tissue and the role of inflammation in arthritis, then taking that knowledge back to treat his patients.

When Charles had a meeting or another reason to be in Washington, he would have lunch with Andy Tkach in the White House dining room. Once the postmaster general was there too and complained about his arthritis. Charles advised him to consult a Washington rheumatologist he respected. For many years rheumatology was a specialty on the fringes, and patients were often not referred appropriately when they could have been helped. When Charles lunched at the White House, the butler would give him a cigar with the White House logo on its band, which he passed along to a delighted Wasil.

I was accepted on the psychiatry staff at the same hospital,

Fairview General, and juggled a slowly increasing schedule of private patients (I used Charles's office) and a couple half days a week at the Veteran's Administration Hospital and one of the community mental health clinics, along with running the household.

Charles took on the job of shopping and cooking on weekends, although the cooking he really enjoyed was special meals for guests. (When we lived in Franklin County, after each baby in days when medical practitioners treated each other free of charge ("professional courtesy"), we invited the obstetrician and his wife for a dinner of Charles's borsch and beef à la Stroganoff.)

In this way he relieved me of some of the 105 meals normally consumed in a week by a family of five. On Saturday morning he would make "blinyi," thin Russian pancakes similar to French crêpes. The children spent Saturday mornings helping in the kitchen and learning from him. They all acknowledged that cooking was not my métier. I could only work in the kitchen with everyone else out, while I windmilled from refrigerator to cupboard to sink to stove to table and around again.

※

Our move to the Cleveland area put us closer to Charles's family in Ellwood City, where we always went to prepare for school in the fall, because Pennsylvania does not have sales tax on clothes. I happened to be working on my Mensa book during the holiday season, when Charles offered me a gift that, while typical of his willingness to help in my projects, impressed my friends in my writing workshop. He offered me a hundred hours of babysitting time so I could work in peace and quiet. By this he meant that he would take the children for several weekends to visit his family. This was a win-win-win-win situation. Not only did it help me but also his family enjoyed having them, the children enjoyed going, and Charles got to eat without me trying to keep his weight down. (I have been happy that Timothey has adopted this idea and brings his children to Rocky River some weekend days to give Patricia time to herself. I take them to dinner, and then they return to Pittsburgh.)

When Munya's husband, Paul, died, she moved back to the house on Glen Avenue where Charles grew up with Wasil and Evdokiya and the other children. The cluttered old house was very welcoming, and the boys liked to go without me because they let them watch television (cartoons and kid-friendly non-educational fare that I didn't allow) and indulge in candy, which they had just one day a month at home, on Candy Day. So going to Ellwood was a big deal.

Christopher Denko wrote:

Ellwood City's Food Circuit

One thing I noticed about Ellwood was how many people knew Pop. We couldn't walk down the street without "Hey, Doc, how are ya?" "Hey, Chuck, long time." "Dr. Denko, where have you been?" *Everyone* knew Pop. (Just like his Dad. When we went to Grandpa's funeral, half the town showed up. They were pouring out the doors of the church waiting to pay their respects.)

The first place we always stopped was the Sinclair station owned by the Italian guy Ralph DiBlasio. We would gas up from the trip, and Pop would catch up on the latest talk around town. This guy really liked Pop. I think he liked the fact that even though Pop was a doctor in the big city far away, he would still buy his gas right there in Ellwood and be interested in the goings-on around town.

Sometimes we would stop at the National Lunch on Main Street. This place had not changed since 1944. With its long countertop and bar stools, we would line up and order the specialty, chilidogs. Now I haven't had a chilidog in twenty years, but I remember those as being exceptionally good. Everyone in there knew Pop too. They would ask about Cleveland, but they really liked to talk about Ellwood. Pop would always humor them.

So after a full day of shopping and eating, we were always just in time to return to Grandma's for a huge meal of whatever she spent all day in the kitchen preparing. The food was universally delicious, but it was never possible to eat enough to keep everyone happy. "Have more, have more, you're a growing boy." "What, you don't like? You only ate three, what's the problem?" "Just one more, it's good for you!" Sometimes it's hard to say no to Grandma, especially when she's making me a meatball I can't refuse.

We comparison-shopped Protestant churches (my background) in Rocky River and neighboring suburbs, but found them cold and unwelcoming, unlike the Gahanna Community Church. Charles suggested that we try an Eastern Orthodox Church (his background), so we went to Sts. Peter and Paul Russian Orthodox Church in Lakewood. I never cared for the stylized antiphonal chanting back and forth between priest and choir because it sounded as though they kept rudely interrupting each other. What Charles and I agreed was exceptional there was the religious instruction program for the children, run by a public school principal and even giving out report cards! In fact years later when our boys represented their high school on their respective Academic Challenge teams, they were the only contestants on their own team or the other who knew any and all the Old Testament answers. (I assume that questions were limited to the Old Testament because of the Jewish contestants, but if there were any Jewish contestants, they did not score points on the religion section.) River teams won each time. In Timothey's year an advanced playoff was instituted, and River won that too.

There were other fringe benefits to belonging to Sts. Peter and Paul that we had not anticipated. A number of members were still second- or third-generation immigrants who were highly skilled tradesmen. If we needed repairs around the house, they always had a first-class craftsman to do the job.

Another advantage became apparent several years after we moved to Cuyahoga County. Helen Balog, the young children's teacher, and her husband, Jim, who had run a folk dancing group when their daughter was of the right age, were resident managers of a twenty-nine-unit apartment building, built in the '30s and looking like a movie set, with paneled mirrors in the entryway and a party room in the basement. They knew it was going on the market and hoped the new owner would keep them on and be congenial to work with. Jim came to Charles to promote the idea. We looked at the building, the books, and the price, all of which were acceptable, so Charles again went to the bank to "play Monopoly" with the banker by moving our securities from our box to the bank's. In this way we bought Parkview Apartments with a first and second mortgage, no money down. We paid off the second quickly; the first took a few years longer, but the payments were all out of rental income. Since Charles ran the securities investments, and since my father had been in real estate so I had heard discussions about renting, I took over working with the Balogs. Helen's books always balanced to the penny. I planned large projects for the summer months when utility bills were small. We had a waiting list for many years, and had only an occasional eviction. Once we had a rejected lover shooting through the window at the object of his affections, and I had to hire a detective to protect her from the driveway on that side. We had that building for thirty years, and it was kind of fun. It satiated the monkey on our backs: travel.

Parkview Apartments also had fringe benefits. Not only did Jim consider minor breakdowns a personal challenge for him to fix but he did them in our house as well. He watched our house when we traveled. (Once we had left it unlocked as we left for Europe, because of not being in the habit of locking up, but Jim closed it up for us.) Better yet, we used the party room for children's birthday parties and for our parties that Charles called my "soirées," where we showed travel slides and had a late-night supper catered by Helen. Our friends and physicians who took care of the children used to ask when the next party would be.

We wanted the children to attend the good public schools of Rocky River with neighborhood children, but I maintained that what was taught in school had to be augmented, so I looked for other children's programs. Charles and Christopher continued with Indian Guides, and Charles joined with each of the others when each reached the appropriate grade. In fact when Nicholas joined, the father of his friend, Doug Berg, lived too far away to join, so we talked the Y into making an exception and letting Doug come as Nicholas's Indian brother. Charles described having two pairs of fumbling hands to help with lacing wallets while the other fathers got impatient. When the boys went on to Scouts, Charles also helped the Scoutmasters. In those days Boy Scouts eschewed having women help, but as volunteers dried up they had to relax that rule. One year I ran the greens sale. With no more than a moderate push from me, and a carrot in the form of a promised trip to the Scout Camp in Philmont, New Mexico, once they made it, they all eventually received their Eagle. Following the suggestion of Margaret Barlow, a blind friend of mine in Mensa, Christopher had an interesting project: he tape-recorded children's books. Once recorded, including his name as reader, they "cloned" the recording for all the schools for the blind in the state.

I also found, in Bay Village, a nearby suburb, the Lake Erie Junior Nature and Science Center, the second such in the country, with classes and opportunities to help care for animals, and all three boys became junior curators. I have always wished I had mastered another language, so I gave the boys chances to learn. I arranged Russian classes for Christopher and a friend with a woman in our church, until she moved to another state. For Nicholas I found a children's conversational French class at Case Western Reserve University, where by the end of the summer they were taking parts in fairy tales, entering and dropping out in the various parts on being tapped by the teacher. Timothey had French one summer with a teacher from our middle school after he had had her in class.

I found Peter Pan Players, a drama school run by a talented local woman. Our boys were all in their respective classes there. Christopher had the part of Peter Zenger, a Colonial printer who promoted freedom of the press. Timothey had the role of *The Tiniest Heart* in the play by that name, about a family of playing cards. Nicholas's teacher wanted him for that part too, but of course Timothey was tinier.

When I observed that they no longer teach grammar (How

can they? The teachers no longer know it), I undertook one summer to spend an hour each morning teaching Nicholas and Timothey the rudiments where the school had left off, after subjects and verbs. We progressed through moods, transitive and intransitive verbs (i.e., the difference between "lie" and "lay") to infinitives, participles, and gerunds, and finally diagramming, so they could visualize sentence structure. A month after Timothey started French in middle school, he told us at dinner, "Mrs. Morrow used to say, 'Class, who can tell us what an infinitive is?' Now she just says, 'Timothey, tell the class what an infinitive is.'" I made sure they all took the two years of Latin the high school offered (although in a watered-down form, without long marks), again as a way to understand the structure of language. Many years later, when Timothey was a resident in psychiatry, he had rounds with a psychiatrist who always opted to stay for coffee with him and talk about language. He envied Timothey for having had me teach him about words and grammar.

❄

When the two younger boys were in middle school, one came home with an assignment to list all the units of measure he could think of, besides the well-known English and metric units, so the four of us sat around the table thinking up such units: watts, ohms, coulombs, faradays, pascals, calories, angstroms, light years. "*Li*, a Chinese measure of distance, is a word Scrabble players use," I told the boys.

"My father used to talk about *versts*, two-thirds of a mile in Russia," Charles commented. With a twinkle in his eye, he added, "Ask your teacher if he knows what a millihelen is."

I bit. "A millihelen? I never heard of that. What's a millihelen?"

"Beauty sufficient to launch one ship—mine."

Theo Moll, a neighbor and self-made industrialist, immigrant from Germany and on the board at Fairview, had been influential in getting Charles for the Scott Research Laboratory. He was also helpful in getting us settled and acquainted. He manufactured small vehicles, bicycles, snowmobiles, tractors, etc., and kept a farm out in Medina County, where we were always invited and could play on his products. (He also gave our boys age-appropriate tricycles and a bicycle.) We could watch the milking, or just rest in the sun, or go fishing in the pond.

One day Charles and Christopher were fishing, and there was a sudden splash. As I was rushing to jump in, Charles caught Timothey by a combination of his clothes and hair. Relieved over an averted tragedy but frightened over what might have been, Charles bawled Timothey out for falling in. I sat there trembling because we should not have had him on the pier at his tender age in the first place. (Timothey later told me he was trying to see the fish. We soon thereafter had him in glasses, but that wouldn't have helped him see fish in the muddy pond.) This was the final of a handful of close calls by all three boys that kept me in a state of constant tension over what would be the next brush with death by one of them. I was never completely relaxed until they were safely asleep.

One evening a call came for Charles from Carl Zerke, a friend from his Ellwood City school days, who was living in Florida. Carl told Charles about his latency-aged grandson's medical problems. Several physicians had been unable to diagnose the problem or offer help. Charles listened, asked a few questions, and said, "I think I can help him. Have Bianca bring him to Cleveland."

Within a few days the child was on the pediatric ward, where Charles talked to his grandmother, examined the boy, and wrote his orders. The boy's condition was a rare autoimmune disease called scleroderma, meaning "hard skin." Scarlike tissue appears on the skin, and the cells lining the walls of small arteries are also damaged. On Charles's treatment the boy improved and was able to return to Florida where Charles coordinated his treatment with their pediatrician. The Zerke family was understandably very appreciative of Charles's help. When Bianca and I had chatted, I told her that when a pharmaceutical company had given Venus flytrap plants to psychiatrists as advertising, I had asked for enough for all our son's classmates who were studying carnivorous plants. Imagine my surprise when Bianca then sent me pitcher plants from her area, another of the carnivorous plants, and a kind that Timothey and I saw later when we went to Borneo primarily to see orangutans.

Later Bianca sent our children a baby caiman. I had thought this was a variety of alligator because they have alligators in Florida; however, on looking it up I found that caimans are neither alligators nor crocodiles, but similar to both. It had to be fed flies or bits of raw hamburger. One day Nicholas held it up to the light to get a better look, and it nipped his nose! How many have survived the bite of a reptile similar to alligators and crocodiles? But we were inexperienced and unable to raise it. I wish I had thought to give it to the nature center, where the boys had classes. They could have saved it, but then what could they have done with a grown caiman? Probably given it to the Cleveland Zoo.

As an adult, after the death of his grandparents, that young man wrote to Charles to express his appreciation for his life-saving help.

❋

In November 1969, when Nicholas was almost five, Charles was scheduled to give a paper at the European Congress in Prague. Having traveled well in Mexico, Christopher would definitely be going. I had been worrying about Nicholas, who had been wearing glasses since age three for "high myopia" and the problems it might cause in the future. I contended that he should see as much as possible as soon as possible, and that meant including him on the European trip. Also, I did not know how long the old-fashioned cross-Atlantic sailings would be available, as in the pre-flight days, and I wanted the boys to experience at least one of these. In those days the large liners served enormous meals, particularly the SS *France*, with its reputation for high cuisine, and for reasons of timing we took that ship for our return. We, of course, signed on for the early seating. Still, their enormous twenty-course dinners dragged on, and Nicholas could not stay awake, but he didn't want to miss any of the fun. He resented it if we commented on how sleepy he was and that perhaps we should get him back to the cabin. Charles would carry him out as the next diners were arriving. To avoid insulting him and hurting his feeling by referring to his fatigue, the three of us would talk in our code by saying how "hungry" he was. The approaching second-seating diners would look astonished that anyone could leave that dining room hungry.

Disembarking in Bremerhaven and taking the train south, I realized that we must pass through Bremen, known by the children for the fairytale "The Town Musicians of Bremen," about four animals forming a pyramid. With Eurailpasses at that time one could jump on and off the trains at will by just showing the conductor the pass. I figured that Bremen must exploit that unusual feature of the story by putting a statue in the town square, so we jumped off to look for it. Actually we saw dozens of renderings of those four animals each on the back of the other—and jumped back on the next train.

❋

After a stop in Basle for Charles to see a colleague and for us to go to the zoo to see the Przewalski's (pronounced shuh-val-skee) horses, bred back to their Mongolian forebears, we routed ourselves to Brno, Czechoslovakia, to visit the monastery where Gregor Mendel had founded the science of genetics by studying dominant and recessive inheritance in peas, from the number of pink blossoms that occurred when plants with red blossoms and those with white blossoms were cross-fertilized. The monk in charge was delighted with our interest and showed us Mendel's desk and garden. This linking of science, history, and geography was beyond even nine-year-old Christopher, not to mention five-year-old Nicholas. We explained it to them later.

During the meeting in Prague, one thing that impressed me was the tremendous population pressure. On sidewalks I would have to hold one child securely in each hand, not to have them washed away by the flood of people. I worried that if it was this bad so soon after the war, what would it and our country be like in a few years. (A few years later I saw what it was like in China, with torrents of bicycles glutting the streets.)

A wives' tour to Orlik Castle was announced, and so I took the children. To my horror, that castle was filled to the rafters with "trophies." Not only were there stuffed animals that had been shot but there were cabinets full of single feathers from birds, since there was no space for the entire bird. The nobleman had evidently intended to bring whole species to extinction. It was ghastly. I had no way to get the children back to Prague except to stay with the tour.

Years later when Christopher was traveling from Prague to Vienna, someone offered to take him to a castle. As they approached, he had a feeling of déjà vu. He asked to have a guide brought to the door and inquired whether the interior contained such remnants of slaughtered animals. She was surprised at the accuracy of his descriptions, and he realized that this was, in fact, the same castle. He refused to enter.

Once in Central Europe, everyone made a fuss over Nicholas and called him, with his golden curls, "*zlaty* Nikolai" (golden Nicholas). In Prague Charles took Christopher, Nicholas, and the daughter of a friend to the Moscow Circus while I went to the opera. Let Charles tell about it:

> During that period the victorious allies strove to demonstrate their close friendship. Their organizational leaders wanted to show off Czechoslovakian recovery from the ravages of World War 2. Therefore they permitted the almost unheard-of presentation of the great, the fabulous Moscow Circus in a non-Communist venue.
>
> I wanted to take our two sons, Christopher and Nicholas, and the near-teenaged daughter of a friend. (Joanne went to the opera.)
>
> At the ticket booth, in a lighthearted tone and my best Russian, I said, "I want four of your best seats."
>
> Guess what—I got them! They were in the center of the main section, two or three rows roped off,

level with the large stage. The stage held an ice rink on which several large brown bears darted back and forth skating, actually successfully playing ice hockey! I wondered who helped them put on their skates.

Looking over my right and left shoulders, I saw that the rest of the roped-off section was occupied by Russian military officers with their shoulder boards jutting out. They were smiling amiably, and it was plain that the Russians had been instructed to be on friendly terms with the locals. I talked with several of them in broken Russian and English, and noticed their stainless steel teeth.

As intermission approached, the buzz of conversation suddenly quieted. The Russian commissar and his underlings (including one woman officer), with their painted ladies, had arrived, and it turned out we had been given their seats. It appeared that this had been done intentionally to embarrass the Russian contingent. The circus came to a halt while all eyes were on how the Russians would handle the sticky situation. But the Russians were not to be outdone by the Czech pranksters. The commissar immediately took in the fact that an American and three children were enjoying the clowns' tricks. He held a quick consultation with the ushers, while the Czech locals obviously enjoyed the discomfiture of the Russian officers.

But, not to be outdone, the commissar quickly turned the situation to his advantage by asking for four more chairs to be brought and inviting us to join their group. The locals recognized that they had been "hoist on their own petard," and the circus continued with the excellent acts for which they are noted.

> By the end of the circus, the Russians had thawed,
> shook hands cordially, and wished us *do svidaniya!*

After the meeting in Prague, on our way to the Tatras, the train stopped for a few minutes in Košiçe. Always one to notice billboards, Charles drew my attention to a poster of a Neanderthal skull. Unable to read the printing from the train window, we agreed it must mean the local museum had one. At a time when Eurail passes allowed you to jump on and off trains at will, we jumped off, took a taxi, and saw one of the rare specimens, then caught the next train. Years later, we explained that tiny skull to the boys.

We headed through the old Jugoslovia to board our ship in Trieste. Ljubljana was where we took the boys to their first opera, Puccini's *Turandot,* which the soloists each sang in his or her preferred language. We were supposed to know the story anyway. The boys liked it when they carried the failed suitor's head on a pike.

That night Nicholas had severe abdominal pain, and we feared appendicitis. Charles called a rheumatologist he had met at the meeting, who referred us to a surgeon. Nicholas was on the gurney on his way to the OR when he vomited and was cured. Acute gastroenteritis is a differential diagnosis with appendicitis, and you operate if in doubt because a ruptured appendix is worse than needless surgery. It was probably that rich Mediterranean seafood casserole. Nicholas still has his appendix.

For the return we boarded ship in Trieste. Ashore in Athens, we showed the boys the Acropolis and tried to instill its significance into their minds. A dock strike in Naples gave us a day to visit Herculaneum.

Our trip had been almost more than little Timothey could bear. He told his Auntie Helen "My mommy isn't coming home anymore." The next day we arrived, and he jumped into my arms.

Back home, our family life orbited around school activities, while Charles continued his work coordinating patient care, animal research, teaching, and learning, and I continued to treat psychiatric patients.

⁂

In 1972 I decided that we should take a trip determined by destination, without a meeting. I wanted to visit Alaska, so we took a family vacation of the kind Charles called "without slides." We traveled up and down the Alcan Highway to Alaska. Charles and I slept in a pop-up tent on top of the station wagon, and the boys pitched pup tents. Like other dirty tourists, we bathed in Liard Hot Springs, going and coming. We also stayed in a motel every few days to get a good bath and a good rest, at the then-exorbitant price of $80 a night for the five of us. At Watson Lake, we made a sign of the distance from Rocky River (2930 miles) by burning it onto firewood, and posted it with hundreds of others.

In Mount McKinley National Park (now Denali) on a brilliant day without cloud cover, we rode the shuttle to within sight of the mountain for which the park is named. We stopped to watch Toklat grizzlies, brown with blond tips, and ptarmigan, already changing to their white winter plumage. While Charles kept the little boys in camp, eleven-year-old Christopher and I climbed higher than and downwind of Dahl sheep, to the ranger's astonishment, when we told him about it.

We crossed east into the Yukon over a highway like a gravel heap to Dawson and Jack London country, where we prospected for gold on a stake the tourist bureau took out for tourists. Drama majors presented readings of Robert Service ("poet of the Yukon") and from London's life and works. They included the anecdote that London had suffered a bout of scurvy over the winter, "cured" by raw potatoes and a can of tomatoes. Charles had treated scurvy in a homeless man on Chicago's west side and concluded that if London's condition had been scurvy, this would not have been enough to cure him. On the same diet, the other three men who overwintered in the cabin with London would have developed the same symptoms but didn't. Knowing the story was medically wrong, Charles became a rheumatologic detective to delve into Jack London's life and medical history. Over the following twenty years, whenever his work took him to California, he pursued clues about London's mysterious illness: a medical chart from London's hospitalization for an appendectomy, London's second wife's diary about his medical problems, and George Sterling's biography.

When London died, the December 14, 1916 *San Francisco Examiner* said London had died of uremic poisoning, or kidney failure. Charles saw the cause of death as lupus, an autoimmune disease that causes damage to any part of the body, including the kidneys. A healthy immune system fights off viruses, bacteria, fungi, and protozoa. When it cannot tell the difference between foreign invaders and healthy tissue, the immune system creates autoantibodies that attack healthy tissue, causing inflammation and pain. Various organs are affected. In the early twentieth century, only a handful of physicians would have been likely to consider the diagnosis of lupus, but London consulted his hunting physician friends instead of those at the cutting edge of medicine.

Charles wrote:

On a brief sojourn in the Klondike Gold Rush in 1897–98, twenty-two-year-old Jack London lived on the common camp menu of bread, beans, and bacon. He reported that he developed scurvy from lack of vegetables and fruit. His self-diagnosis was based on features of the "Klondike Plague," namely bleeding, swollen gums, and painful joints. None of London's companions on the same diet shared the symptoms. A cabin mate, Dr. B. F. Harvey, urged London to leave since he believed that there was no cure in the Yukon, although native Canadians had for centuries empirically brewed tea from pine needles for an extract that prevented and treated the disease because it contained vitamin C.

London's bout of "severe scurvy" was better explained as an attack of acute lupus involving the mouth and joints. After returning to Oakland, London required medical attention for mouth and tooth care through 1899. At that time it was unlikely his mouth and dental problems were another manifestation of scurvy since he ate a normal California diet.

London married his second wife, Charmian, who kept a diary of his illnesses until the end of his life. At one point he was unable to pass the medical examination for insurance. Charmian noted that London, at age twenty-eight, suffered severe headaches. When London was thirty-two, Charmian described a bad case of facial pain, one of the common signs of lupus. London also suffered repeated pulmonary problems, grippe, bronchitis, colds, and chest pain. In 1914, aboard the military transport *Ossabow* to cover the Mexican Revolution, he was diagnosed to have pleurisy, a painful inflammation of the membrane around the lungs, which is another place lupus often strikes.

Skin symptoms are also common in lupus, especially when one is exposed to much sun. London had recurrent sun rashes. After four hours in the sun he developed huge swollen blotches that defied explanation by his physician. His throat was swollen so badly he was unable to swallow water.

In the South Pacific at age thirty-two, he experienced itching and swollen and painful hands followed by peeling of the skin. His toenails grew exceedingly thick as they do with psoriasis and lupus. Rheumatic symptoms were repeatedly described in Charmian's diary. In 1904, she noted that London had such severe pain in his knees and ankles that he had to be at bed rest for sixty-five hours. This followed the minor trauma of jumping down three feet onto a round stick.

In 1908 in the South Pacific during London's months-long bout of dermatologic disorders, he also suffered fever, rash with hives, malaise, headache, facial pain, and even a bout of delirium. He dealt with his anxiety and pain by chain-smoking, and took opiates for his diarrhea and quinine for his fever, which he believed was caused by malaria. Coincidentally, a derivative of quinine was one of the early treatments for lupus, so he had the right treatment for lupus but the wrong diagnosis for his symptoms—or he may have had malaria too.

I looked at photographs of Jack London for more clues. In one picture taken during his last year of life, London is shown working on a manuscript, both his hands clearly visible. The left hand shows the thumb bent back too far, spindling of the index finger, and swollen middle finger. The right hand has a swollen knuckle at the base of the fourth finger. The final picture he posed for in 1916 shows the right hand with a swollen knuckle, this time at the base of the second finger. This kind of scattered joint involvement is typical of lupus.

London had repeated bouts of fever diagnosed as malaria. In 1908, he wrote in a letter, "Fever cures about everything else a man has." It was the *treatment* for the fever that helped him.

He must have received antimalarial drugs, such as quinine, a modern treatment for lupus, and the other symptoms responded without anyone knowing the relationship. In 1913, at age thirty-seven, London was found to have kidney disease. Charmian reports he had an operation to remove his appendix, and afterward his physician told him his kidneys were in terrible shape.

The most likely explanation for London's death remains an abdominal complication of lupus. He was working, writing, as was his custom. Obviously, death was not regarded as imminent by his physician, his wife, his family at the ranch, or himself. I believe that an abdominal complication that had been reported to cause sudden death in lupus was responsible.

When his travels took him to California, Charles tracked down Charmian's diary, examined London's hospitalization records, and even visited Becky, the remaining of London's two daughters by his first marriage, in a nursing home where, he noted:

She showed me family pictures of her father. "Did he have much trouble with arthritis?" I asked, having seen several swollen finger joints in a later photograph.

She said, "It's funny you should ask. The last two years of his life he had a lot of trouble walking because of pain and swelling in his feet."

Author George Sterling had attributed London's death to suicide by morphine overdose. While London had used morphine by prescription to obtain relief from abdominal pain, at his death a vial was found containing four pills. People intent on suicide usually take all the pills. London's physicians administered treatment without success, including stomach pumping.

Becky was delighted to learn that her father had not died an alcoholic death or committed suicide but suffered from lupus. This gave the loyal daughter the peace she had wanted for years.

By 1974 Charles had earned a six-month sabbatical. He had two invitations: to a government spa in Czechoslovakia run by a friend, or to Australian National University (ANU) in Canberra, the best of new postwar universities, with Dr. Michael Whitehouse. Charles had met Michael in Columbus, and he and his wife and children had visited us in Rocky River. The men continued corresponding after the Whitehouses had gone on to Australia. One advantage for Charles at the spa was virtually unlimited access to the blood of patients with many kinds of arthritis. Several advantages were inherent in the Australian invitation: a new country and continent, the use of English, the chance to live in a foreign capital, observe Australian life, and return home with a new perspective. We had to leave Whitefoot behind, our only surviving dog, in Charles's lab.

Our adventure began before leaving the States. We camped across the Southwest to show the boys the Painted Desert, Petrified Forest, and Grand Canyon. The final night before embarking at Los Angeles, we camped at Joshua Tree National Park. With twenty-seven suitcases we boarded the *Oriana* for our twenty-day crossing, which was leisurely because of days at several ports, the first of which was San Francisco. We took the boys to see the Coast Redwoods in Muir Woods. The next stop was Oahu, and as luck would have it the date was December 7, Pearl Harbor Day. Charles took the boys to the ceremony at the sunken USS *Arizona* at Pearl, while I spent most of the day at the Polynesian Cultural Center.

The next day ashore was in Fiji, where a bagpiple band on the pier welcomed us. We then stopped in Auckland, New Zealand, and visited their museum where we saw the skeleton of a moa, an extinct flightless bird up to twelve feet tall.

This was the first time for any of us to cross the equator, with all its King Neptune frivolities: throwing raw liver and pushing each other into the pool. My moment of greatest excitement came one dark night when on deck I identified two hazy glowing oval patches in the sky, the Greater and Lesser Magellanic Clouds. These are small sister galaxies of our Milky Way Galaxy, visible to the naked eye only in the Southern Hemisphere. With arms extended I could cover them with my thumbs, and I called them the giant thumbprints of God. Another sight was the unimpressive Southern Cross, so beloved by denizens of the Southern Hemisphere.

Another enjoyable feature of the trip was meeting Lorna Curtin, wife of the Australian ambassador to England. At a shipboard Scrabble party she recognized I would be a good opponent. We played a tournament across the Pacific; each of us won the same number of games, but Lorna's margins were always greater than mine. We later visited the Curtins in Sydney. Their son suffered a malignant melanoma (as do many Aussies, from living under that glaring sun), and Charles's input helped his treatment.

Finally we arrived in Sydney harbor and were met by our host, Michael, who drove us to Canberra. While in Australia, Charles was invited to lecture at various universities and also to become an honorary member of the Australian Rheumatologic Association. He treasured his ARA necktie.

Charles and Michael and a chemist, Ray Walker, worked on how copper can help soft-tissue irritations of various kinds. They developed a copper-containing ointment for external use called Alcusal.

Despite Canberra's excellent public transportation, we needed a car. The secondhand one we bought had typical sun-damaged finish, making me think of it as sunburned. For a couple weeks it took three of us to get anywhere, one on the controls, one on the map, and Christopher yelling, "Keep left!" Charles noticed that Aussie men typically drove the one family car to work, parked it for the day, and drove home, while their wives shopped at the baker's, the butcher's, and the greengrocer's on foot and staggered home laden with provisions. They shopped for groceries *every day!* I drove Charles to and from the university each day and used the car for errands.

We had timed our arrival to coincide with Christmas and their summer vacation. (One of their songs began, "You know it's Christmastime when the red fern blooms.") I asked how

Aussie children spent their vacations. For Christopher I found a drama group, into which he was accepted, given a part, and traveled to perform in the outback. For the little boys I found a day camp at a park where one of the play devices consisted of a pulley with handles, on a wire, for gliding down a slope just above the ground. It was called a "flying fox," the name given to a large bat we would see at night, looking like a piece of newspaper being flapped through the night sky by the wind.

By spring the children started school, Christopher in third form (ninth grade), the others in third and second grade, but they were immediately, on the first day, both advanced a grade.

While in Australia, we made a point to encounter and learn about their aboriginal population. In a shopping mall near our flat was an aboriginal art shop run by Rohan, a woman who lived with aboriginal locals who had even ritually adopted her. She had aboriginal buyers around the country who knew the art she wanted and sent her shipments of aboriginal work. "It's like Christmas when it comes," she told me.

The paintings, usually on bark, were highly stylized and symbolic, with channels with sharp bends, not naturalistic curves, representing watercourses, water being very important in the desert. The colors were desert tones and black from natural pigments. Certain artists were well known, and their work in demand by museums. As the artists aged, they developed cataracts from the desert sun despite their dark-brown eyes, and experts noticed the decline in their work. I picked out several paintings to bring home to Rocky River.

I was more interested in their decorated objects for everyday use. I don't think the children ever got the hang of throwing the boomerang. Our didgeridoo is a decorated trunk of a small sapling hollowed out by burning. We were never able to inhale through the nose and at the same time exhale through the mouth, blowing on the end to produce a constant tone, which the locals could do for hours.

The most interesting things I bought from Rohan were a pair of kurdaitja shoes, a shaman's or witchdoctor's shoes. They are made of emu feathers and human hair, rolled into a strong fiber on the thigh of the woman making them. The shoes are oval-shaped at both ends and held on by an ankle strap. This makes the prints the same at both ends so the track does not reveal the direction the shaman takes as he goes about his ritual duties, which include murder. These were said to be of museum quality, but Rohan had no buyer but me. When I showed them at our Australian soirée or on other occasions, asking people to guess what they were, the most frequent speculation was "birds' nests?"

Instead of seeing patients, I joined the bush-walking wives' club. I saw an echidna, one of the two monotremes (egg-laying mammals), in the bush as it ran to hide in a hollow tree. On family rides within a few miles of Canberra we saw many kangaroos and koalas munching eucalyptus leaves up in trees. We saw also the emu, Australia's large flightless bird, which shares space opposite the kangaroo on Australia's escutcheon. In the lake at the center of Canberra, we saw the other monotreme, a platypus swimming, looking like a beaver with a duck's bill.

Realizing that six months would go by very quickly, I instituted a "one sightsee a weekend" policy, which included the typical pioneer cabin brought to Canberra and the astronomy station at Tidbinbilla. We saw one of the four extant copies of the Magna Carta (1215). They indicated that it delineated for the first time that women had a legal right in England. It was compensation if someone killed her husband, thereby cutting off her support. (In ancient Rome there were several other rights assigned to women, including the right for a female slave *not* to be raped by her owner. For all the good that right probably did.)

Over a long Easter weekend we saw one of the marvels of Australia, the Great Barrier Reef. We took the train north along the coast, visited Brisbane's horticultural gardens, and proceeded north to Green Island, one of the main sites for viewing the reef. The glass-bottomed boat didn't help much because we rocked so much with the waves, but I was enthralled with the life we could see by just walking on the dead reef, not fish in the shallow waters but lower life forms, vivid cobalt-blue starfish and pink sea cucumbers that looked like blobs of bubblegum.

In Mackay we met Mila Hoagland, a Dutch physician who with her husband had left the Dutch East Indies when they were lost by Holland, and established a family practice in Australia. Mila took us to a place where we could see living coral opening and closing their polyps as they fed from the nutrient-rich ocean soup, and retracting into their sheaths when startled by our approach. Like Charles with his interest in stamps with maps, Mila specializes in stamps with sea life, which Australia issues in abundance.

Mila and her husband took us into the outback. Charles wrote:

Our friends drove us on the Atherton Escarpment to a small town somewhat deserted, and on to the desert where an enormous rock juts out of the sand, about a hundred feet high, a half mile long, and a quarter mile broad at ground level. The lower part of this rock is covered with painted figures representing animal and human characters. Each day the setting sun is reflected in brilliant colors. It is like a miniature version of Ayers Rock.

The habitat of the natives is primitive, a windbreak of various plants and sheets of building material. Several such structures each surround a fire, and each fire is surrounded by men, women, and children lounging about. Several white men chatted nearby. "We are the Flying Doctors of North Australia providing medical care to these people. Would you like to know more about them? We are flying out tomorrow."

We had to decline because we had no one with whom to leave the children, and their plane was small.

Another long trip was to Alice Springs and Ayers Rock. We took the train to Adelaide in the south, then up the center of the continent, past wild camels imported in hopes of using them in the desert. We all climbed Ayers Rock, which glows at sundown and is a religious site for the aborigines, the home of "Rainbow Serpent." When we were there, they had a plague of marsupial mice, but I didn't think to dissect one. The newborn must be the size of a flea for a litter to fit into the mother's pouch.

As the time came to leave Australia, we returned to Sydney, visited the zoo, where we saw the tree-climbing marsupial from Papua New Guinea, and boarded the *Oronsay,* a sister ship of the *Oriana.* The stops were the same as those outward bound. On Fiji I attended the typical South Sea Islands hotel's night-club act, with waiters walking on glowing coals. The waiter who seated me also invited me to his home island, which I had to decline. The only additional stop on the return voyage was Vancouver, where we took the boys to Stanley Park and the collection of Northwest Native American totem poles.

Back in North America, I routed us to the eastern slope of the Sierra Nevada to see bristlecone pines, recently found to be older than the redwoods. They conserve their precious water by growing almost parallel to the ground, sacrificing large parts of their volume to death, but putting out small tufts of cone-bearing new growth, ready to reproduce. As an adult, Nicholas told me that my advance explanations about their great age had led him to expect that they would be larger than the redwoods.

Using our final few days, we visited the Otts, Mensa friends we had met in Columbus, who were house sitting an R and R ranch near Vail, Colorado.

We arrived home with most of the summer ahead of us and a wonderful collection of family memories binding us together.

❈

Having studied copper as an anti-inflammatory agent, Michael and Ray and Charles had found that topical copper compounds were more effective than other agents. Michael, along with chemist Ray Walker, had formulated the copper-based medication Alcusal.

Back home, a few of Charles's arthritis patients volunteered to try Alcusal to treat conditions such as bursitis and tendonitis. Charles gave a sample to a local athletic coach to treat sports injuries, and he reported Alcusal to be superior to any other agent in treating sprains and strains. Tennis elbow responded well, along with insect bites, poison ivy irritation, and muscle pain.

Charles wanted to make and market Alcusal in the USA, and worked on the permissions necessary. He arranged with the Australian company to export Alcusal to the U.S. He submitted a protocol to the Food and Drug Administration, which was acceptable for efficacy trials. Charles soon organized Alcusal of North America, chartered in Pennsylvania, and even bought a small building with plans to manufacture and market the ointment, but his plan fell through due to bureaucratic intransigence. This is unfortunate because Alcusal would have been a good addition to the rheumatologic formulary.

Denko Family
(on Presidents' Day school holiday).

"He made me a problem solver."

—Nicholas Denko

"He made me a problem solver."

—Christopher Denko

"He made me a problem solver."

—Timothey Denko

One of the pleasures of living with Charles was that he was always sharing his observations about rheumatology, both at home and elsewhere. We could be watching the news and he would say, "Just look at Eric Sevareid's hands!" Once, in a museum, he indicated a dinosaur's lumbar spine, and this compassionate clinician said, "What a terrible backache that poor creature must have suffered."

— Joanne Denko

CHAPTER 9

RHEUMATOLOGIC RESEARCH AND PATIENT CARE (1976–1987)

FOLLOWING OUR RETURN from the Australian adventure we spent the next decade getting the children through school and off to higher education. Rocky River had good public schools, but I became aware that the curriculum had become less challenging. I made it a point to instruct them in what I noticed the school was remiss in teaching. One important omission was grammar. One summer Nicholas, Timothey, and I spent the first hour of the day where the school had left off (after subjects and verbs). I took them through parts of speech, transitive and intransitive verbs (those whose action requires an object and those that don't, as in "lay" and "lie"), and moods, through infinitives, participles, and gerunds, and on to diagramming. I expected them to take the two years of Latin that the school offered, again as a way to understand the anatomy of language, but it was less demanding than when I studied it. They never read Vergil.

Christopher graduated from his fifth high school in 1978, started at George Washington University, and transferred to and graduated from American University. During those years there were problems with him, which caused increasing tension among the three of us, Charles, Christopher, and me. That part of his story is told in another book, and we shall pick up his course later, when he began to return to the family.

Soon after coming to Rocky River, I met Charmaine Severson, a talented and accomplished writer, who introduced me to her writers' workshop. From then until the present, in addition to my psychiatric practice I have engaged in writing books, reading portions at that workshop or a poetry workshop, evaluating criticism, improving my work, and eventually publishing my books.

One day Charmaine brought a new member, Deb Glaefke Baldanza, whose face was afflicted with a fiery red splotchy rash. I called her at her home that evening to ask whether her skin problem had been diagnosed. In an article she wrote subsequently for the *Akron Beacon-Journal* about her problems with lupus, she related that she would have replied angrily to anyone else asking such an intrusive question. She swallowed her retort and told me she had suffered many seemingly unrelated problems since her teen years, ranging from a possible heart attack to miscarriages in all but one of several pregnancies. I told her I thought she had lupus, and that she should see the best doctor available for that condition, who just happened to be my husband.

"You know," she said, "a couple other doctors mentioned lupus, but nobody followed through on it."

Charles won her confidence at the first examination. Deb

was tired of hearing that her problems were all due to nerves. "If you can't tell me what's wrong," she told Charles, "I'm going to kill myself."

"That's the stupidest thing I ever heard," he said. Deb started to cry. He patted her hand and said what medical schools don't teach: "Sometimes you have to give up. I promise I'll tell you when that is."

But when I heard this story, I knew better. Charles never gave up on anyone.

A blood test was negative for lupus, but he knew that nothing is specific to lupus. He noticed a high protein level that often accompanies lupus. Being a highly competent clinician who treated patients, not lab results, he was confident that she had the condition and started treating her for it. She improved in a few months and managed to carry a second pregnancy to term. I did not see Deb again because she dropped out of the workshop.

In 1979, the School of Medicine of Erasmus University in Rotterdam invited Charles to serve as a visiting professor in August. Timothey would soon turn thirteen, and since he had not yet experienced an Atlantic crossing, we decided that this would be a good time to take him and Nicholas.

We took the bus to Toronto, where it let us off right at the pier where we boarded the Polish ship *Stefan Batory*, its five-star dining room the only one on the oceans at that time. We enjoyed a thousand-mile cruise down the St. Lawrence River before heading into the Atlantic, passing the brilliantly lighted Quebec City at night. I happened to be on deck at the right time to see an enormous pod of dozens of whales in the Gulf of St. Lawrence.

Part of the entertainment was a quiz game targeted at passengers of Polish descent, since the ship accommodated travel to and from Poland. Charles was in the lead until the final question, "What is the name of the village where Chopin was born?" To everyone's amazement Charles produced a version, which he admitted was mangled, of *Zhelazova Vola.* (Charles always knew that sort of thing, and no one could beat him at Trivial Pursuit. Once my friend Charmaine invited us over for the four of us to play Trivial Pursuit, but Charles had the first turn and was still answering everything right half an hour later, so the rest of us gave up.) Zhelazova Vola was, in fact, the name of the estate where Chopin's father made the family's living as a tutor for children. (When I visited Zhelazova Vola on another trip, I was shown the alcove in which Chopin's mother delivered the infant Frederic. The Chopin Society keeps fresh flowers there year-round. In 1909 the Russian Sergei Lyapunov composed a symphonic poem by that title to celebrate Chopin's centenary.) For winning the quiz, Charles was awarded a beautiful women's woven green belt, which he gave to me.

We visited the factory that had hidden Anne Frank's family. I choked back tears as I watched a Japanese mother in formal attire help her five-year-old son sign his name in Kanji.

Afterward we returned home on the Russian *MV Mikhail Lermontov*, and Nicholas and I danced the Kalinka.

The following year the Pan American Congress was held in Bogota, Colombia. For years Charles had talked about wanting to travel through Central America by surface to see it as we went, and so, with school out for the summer, the four of us packed and started. Our first stop was San Antonio, Texas, where I took the boys to see the Alamo while Charles bought train tickets. We proceeded south through Mexico by train to Guatemala City. (In the zoo, I had hoped to see a quetzal, the beautiful jungle bird for which the Guatemalan currency is named, but it had died.) We continued south by Ticabus (Transit International Centro America), which stopped each night at a hotel, where we could stay as long as we wished and then continue. It catered to middle-class travelers. One sailor, who knew every port on earth like the back of his hand but for whom the interior was a *terra incognita,* had a backpack proclaiming "A Cabo Horno." Another young man was return-ing to Nicaragua and told his seatmate that his country would be needing him. That fall Nicaragua was in civil strife, and I hoped the gentle young man was safe. Our bus was stopped once and Nicholas but not Timothey was patted down, but not Charles, with his bad leg. One border was marked by a river in which women were doing laundry. I watched, trans-fixed, as a meter-long iguana swam in a sinuous wave, from El Salvador to Honduras, my camera around my neck unused.

Our plan was to visit Julio Wong, a friend from medical school, in Panama. Julio's father and other relatives had come from China a couple generations earlier and had done well in Panama City with Chinese restaurants, so well, in fact, that Julio's father had taken his wife and children to Europe for a year in Julio's childhood. Julio took us to see the Panama Canal, where bunting proclaimed the visit of President Carter. We took the seventy-five-minute transcontinental train trip across the Isthmus to Colon, where the S-curve of land makes the sun rise in the Pacific and set in the Atlantic, and beautiful azure butterflies float in the air. Julio was so funny that the boys laughed constantly, and we overstayed our time, necessitating that we fly instead of taking coastal shipping to Colombia, as we had planned.

Our flight climbed, leveled, and landed in the airport of
Bogota, the world's highest capital, where they met us with delicious coffee. The city itself produced culture shock. Everywhere
on the streets were boys of eight or ten, living by their wits. The
highest percentage of *gaminos* in the world was Bogota's shame.
(Little girls also were living on the streets.) Beggars, often old
women, slept in the thick doorways of churches. We saw the
gold museum behind massive time-locked doors in the basement of the main bank. This was our sons' first sight of South
America and of real poverty and destitution. Yet it was not as
bad as the Haiti Charles and I had visited with my parents.

On our return we stopped again with Julio, who had arranged
for Charles to lecture in the University's medical school, where
Julio ran the surgery department. We were impressed that even
Charles's jokes crossed the language barrier, probably helped
by the fact that the students had only English-language texts
from which to study.

❋

Several years after the sabbatical we received a letter from
Don Laycock, president of the Australian Mensa, who, as
well as other members, had been very cordial to us. Don told
us that he was planning a trip around the world, stopping to
lecture in various places on his way to England, and asked if
we would put him up for a few days in Cleveland. In return,
he offered to "sing for his supper," meaning to give a lecture
for whomever we wished. For some reason we didn't receive
his letter until after he had left Australia, but he had listed
his stops and I sent a copy of our welcoming letter to each.
We connected, and Charles and I took separate days to show
him around Cleveland, the Art Museum, the Natural History
Museum, and the European outdoor market. Unfortunately,

our world-renowned Cleveland Orchestra was not performing at Severance Hall. We like to show it off.

Don impressed our boys by showing them his initials under the article on New Guinean languages in our Encyclopedia Britannica, since he is the recognized authority on those languages. The boys also liked it that one night when Charles and I had given up and gone to bed, Don let them stay up with him to watch *Benny Hill.* I am always happy for my children (and now my grandchildren) to have an opportunity to talk to and know intelligent and unusual adults with interesting lives and stories.

We invited our friends to a "soirée" in the party room at Parkview. In the promised lecture Don told us that a fifth of all the world's languages are spoken in New Guinea, some by as few as a couple hundred speakers. He works on dictionaries before these languages are lost. Some even have parts of speech that our language lacks, such as a "postposition," the reverse of a "preposition." He told us about special kinds of languages called pidgins and Creoles, resulting from speakers of different languages coming together and mixing them. To Charles these terms sounded like casseroles.

In 1982 Charles and I joined a People-to-People tour to China, for which we all offered lectures to create a Chinese menu, from which the Chinese hosts interested in pharmacology could select. They educated us about their herbs and plants. They took us to hospitals, to one of which a bicycle-drawn ambulance was bringing a patient, and to factories that were preparing dried pharmacologically active plants. Charles's talk was requested several times, but mostly the Chinese wanted to hear about our then-new insulin pump, from one of the other attendees. My offering on the tests and pharmacology of depression was never chosen because they knew that "no good Communist ever gets depressed," so I was free to go sightseeing instead. We were taken to the standard sights, mostly in and around Beijing. I found Nanking the most interesting, specifically for its Rape of Nanking Massacre Museum, reminding us of the brutal Japanese occupation of that city in 1937. A Chinese man in uniform with no visible connection to pharmacology rode on our bus throughout the tour. We all agreed that he must be a Chinese spy learning what he could from us. When the time came for us to depart, he hugged Charles and called him "brother."

The following year a European Congress was held in Moscow. Charles gave a paper but skipped many of the meetings because their program for the wives was so good that he went with us instead. Of course Charles knew Russian, but the other wives were impressed that I knew the Cyrillic alphabet, could sound out signs, and knew that "pectopaw" meant "restaurant." We visited Lenin's dacha in the country, with the "Russian invention" of the telephone. We were taken to the apartment in a large general hospital where Dostoevsky grew up when his father was the physician in charge. We saw Fyodor's little toy horse on wheels with a pull string. Then we took the post-Congress extension to Leningrad. Knowing that Charles wanted very much to see the Scythian gold collection (from north of the Black Sea) in the basement of the Hermitage Museum, I nagged our guide to get us there, and she tried, but the excuses were incredible: "Only groups of five, not four or six." "Only Monday or Wednesday, not Thursday," etc. But our excellent guide finally managed it. (We were told in Israel that, worldwide, Russian and Israeli guides are the best, and I have no reason to dispute that.) To get into that gold art collection, they made Charles—on his cane—run around the sidewalk of three sides of the enormous museum. I marveled at the craftsmanship 2,000 to 2,500 years ago, with no magnifying instruments. I saw a hedgehog with fine drawn-out quills of gold, and a chariot with angels hovering over it. (Zoroastrian influence? I had read that they were big on angels.) Charles, as usual, located something rheumatologic: a gold bowl with an engraving of a shaman examining the ankle (in a boot) of a patient wincing with pain, both hands clearly showing swelling on various joints as he gripped his staff. Charles showed the picture of the bowl to many rheumatologists, most of whom agreed with Charles's diagnosis of inflammatory arthritis. With Charles Malemud's indispensable help, Charles Denko's final paper, "Artistic Evidence of Inflammatory Arthropathy from Ancient Scythia," has finally (2016) been accepted for publication in the British journal *Archives of Medicine.*

As the younger boys graduated from high school in 1982 and 1983, the parents put on an "all-night" party to keep them off the streets. Early each year a committee called for help to write the funny entertainment, consisting of skits, parodies, and adaptations of popular songs. Most parents who signed on went as couples, but that was not at all my kind of writing, so I let Charles help compose the jokes. I joined the group that performed, and I danced a parody of an honors English teacher I liked and admired very much. I was asked to repeat that dance the following year. That second year I was also in the chorus line, and we danced the Charleston as we twirled our Flapper-era beads.

Charles maintained contact with Christopher, since I had written him off as part of the family, by traveling to Washington every few months. In summer he included Christopher's brothers when possible, thus trying to maintain some semblance of family life, and I credit him for the fact that this probably helped bring Christopher around by the time he was thirty. Years later Christopher, our humorous chronicler, described one such trip:

Summer Fishing, Sort Of

Dad and the boys got together for a late summer fishing trip. They picked me up in Washington, D.C. and headed to Raystown Lake, an Army Corps of Engineers project that was the largest manmade lake in Pennsylvania. The fishing offshore was terrible—all the big ones were out far and deep—but we had a good time setting up camp and wandering around and even fished a little. Nicholas had been a year at the University of Pennsylvania and was going back, and Timothey was about to begin at Kenyon College, so the trip was their last hurrah before school.

We stayed up late at night, sitting around the fire and discussing everyone's plans for the coming year. A man on the site next to ours waited for a group of friends to show up for the weekend. He had so much food, he was happy to share in exchange for a little company. The conversation grew very animated and very late until Dad came out of the RV at one point yelling, "Will you guys shut up! I can't sleep. How are you going to catch fish if you stay up all night?" So we packed it in. Driving back to DC was pretty rough the next day, but Nicholas and Timothey helped out. The next fishing trip was to Kelley's Island in Erie County, Ohio, and when Dad came out to yell, we told him we were going night fishing. He accepted our reason, although he did grumble all the way back to the RV.

❋

Sometimes we invited my friend Charmaine to attend cultural or scientific events with us. The year 1985 was J.S. Bach's tercentennial, and a birthday concert was announced on a cathedral organ. In nurses' training Charmaine had learned to offer support when the way was dark, steep, or uncertain. She wrote:

> The steps to the main doors of the church did not spill leisurely to the sidewalk but had been short-spaced, making the risers higher than the steps. We assaulted the steps like mountaineers, neither wanting to grunt and strain. I sensed the heaviness and effort of Charles's disadvantaged leg; yet his other side was a revelation, light as a Bach fugue.

Several months later, as Charmaine wrote, she again offered Charles her arm on the way to see a comet:

> In the cold winter's night, we walked a field of corn stubble that reared upward to the brow of a ridge where a line of telescopes and binoculars mounted on tripods were focused on Halley's Comet.
>
> We entered the cornfield, then hesitated. Clumpy furrows with tough stalks formed a nightmare staircase to a tangle of spikes at the top. In the darkness, it was a struggle. Our eyes adjusted after several minutes, and we soon climbed with confidence. Charles

was so focused on reaching the top of the ridge that nothing short of a landslide could have stopped him from seeing the comet.

Years later, Charmaine remarked that the treacherous furrows, each more tricky and ankle-turning than the one below, paralleled the challenges of Charles's life, of all that could have stood in his way but had not.

※

One lifetime goal of mine was to set foot on the Antarctic continent, a map of which had appeared on the back flyleaf of my orange Ginn & Co. geography textbook at Lafayette School. "Someday I'm going there," I promised myself.

Charles and I had visited many interesting places, mostly in Europe, as a result of his recurring question, "There's a meeting in, e.g., Reykjavik. Do you want to go?" My standard answer was, "Of course. Submit a paper." These were all cities, often cultural centers, but Reykjavik was one of the few near some of Earth's natural wonders we had yet to arrange to see. I had no way to know how long his or my health would hold up for taking difficult trips. Charles had spotted an ad for a trip to Churchill, on Hudson Bay, to see the polar bears preparing to leave land to float on the ice for the winter to hunt seals, so we signed on. We saw them on the islands from a helicopter and on land from a bus with barred windows. The following winter we went to see seals on the ice on the St. Lawrence.

We were on all the alumni lists (between us we had attended half of the Big Ten schools plus a few private ones) and received announcements of their trips, but sometimes when I would show Charles one of their brochures, he would lay it aside to "think about it."

Therefore I met him one night with *my* question: "Would you like to know what trip with the University of Michigan I've paid a deposit on?"

It was, of course, Antarctica. We had such a calm voyage across the notoriously rough Drake Passage that it gave us time for sixteen shore excursions in Antarctica. Charles did very well, got back and forth to shore in Zodiacs (inflatable boats), visited penguin colonies and research stations (United States's, England's, Poland's, and China's Great Wall Station). Charles missed just two things: climbing the volcano on Deception Island and swimming in the warm effluent at its base. I swam there, but not very long.

In that packed year Charles gave a paper for the European Congress held in Jerusalem. On our post-congress sightseeing, he jumped out of his seat on the bus yelling "Ashqelon!" He asked the driver to stop for him to take a picture of the sign pointing to that ancient city with a rheumatologic connection. Reading the Greek historian Herodotus, who traveled around the civilized world, Charles learned that Herodotus had observed in Ashqelon the condition that millennia later came to be called "rheumatoid arthritis." This was the first literary allusion to a rheumatologic ailment in history that Charles was aware of. Herodotus attributed it to anger of the city's goddess. Charles attributed it to soldiers returning from fighting in Egypt, passing through Ashqelon and leaving genes with the temple prostitutes. The people on the bus, unaware that Charles had spent a lifetime studying arthritis, attributed his excited outburst to some kind of craziness.

As I have often remarked, Charles was never far from making a rheumatologic observation, and this was part of the pleasure of living with him. We were once in a museum in Monaco where they had a dinosaur skeleton. "Just look at those lumbar vertebrae," said this sympathetic clinician. "What a terrible backache that poor creature must have suffered."

In Eilat on the Gulf of Aqaba we learned of a day trip into the Sinai Desert in Egypt to visit St. Catherine's monastery, which had been under the authority of the Eastern Orthodox Church since the early years of the Christian era. They showed us beautiful icons and ancient manuscripts considered comparable to the Gutenberg Bible. They showed us a large, scraggly, nondescript bush that they believe was the source of Jehovah's voice at the time of the Exodus. Also, the tablets of the Ten Commandments were said to have come down from Mount Sinai adjacent to the monastery. I was very intrigued by a "charnel house," or building containing only the skulls of dead monks, when they could no longer bury their entire brother.

That same year Nicholas received two degrees from the University of Pennsylvania in four years, having placed out of the freshman year: a BS and an MA (in education). While practice-teaching in middle school, he arrived one day dressed as Einstein and told the class about relativity. He was offered several opportunities to teach science in middle schools, but he had plans to continue his own scientific career and eventually teach at a graduate level.

Timothey graduated the following year from Kenyon College, then delayed for several years going on to medical school.

In 1987 Charles and I attended a celebration of the centennial of the groundbreaking Michelson-Morley Experiment by Albert A. Michelson, a physicist at the Case School of Applied Science, and Edward W. Morley, a chemist at the Western

Reserve University (now amalgamated as the Case Western Reserve University). By means of light reflected by a mirror spinning at a known (very high) velocity, this experiment demonstrated that light travels at the same speed whether traveling with the rotating Earth or at right angles to it. Scientists in Europe were attempting to demonstrate this phenomenon at the same time. The fact that it was accomplished here put Cleveland on the scientific map.

Eventually we learned that the administration at Fairview had persuaded Mrs. Scott, the widow of the research donor, to change the terms of the bequest, so they could discontinue the Scott Research Laboratory, tear down the building, and use the space for an outpatient surgery building. Charles would no longer have work at or income from Fairview. Would this mean another move?

No. He arranged to stay at Case Western Reserve University full time, without pay. We considered that our final contribution to medicine, this one a financial contribution as well as a research contribution.

At least the timing was such that Charles had completed his rat work and no longer needed animal facilities. He did need cooperation from other rheumatologists in giving him blood from patients with a vast array of rheumatologic ailments, and laboratory facilities and a technician to freeze, store, and study the blood for the waste products from inflammation and arthritis metabolic products. The university provided these.

And we did not need to move again.

Joanne & Charles Denko in their home in Rocky River
(press photo, 1988).

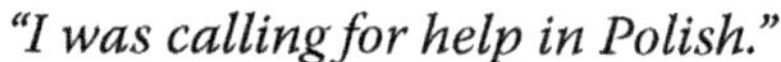

"I was calling for help in Polish."

—Charles, while being mugged in Warsaw

CHAPTER 10

CHARLES'S MOST PRODUCTIVE YEARS (1987–1998)

IN 1982 AND 1983 Nicholas and Timothey had graduated from high school and had left, respectively, for the University of Pennsylvania in Philadelphia and Kenyon College in Gambier, Ohio, the latter as a National Merit Scholar. Thus we were the proverbial "empty nest" parents. This left us without the day-to-day distraction of children at home and we both were free to follow our own schedules. Four years later the boys graduated, and remained away from home, Timothey going to live with Nicholas in Philadelphia while deciding what to do next, and Nicholas continuing to work for a couple years in cancer research at the Wistar Institute in Philadelphia, later going to the University of Cincinnati College of Medicine. Without Charles's office at Fairview, I rented office space nearby to see patients and also went out into the country on Saturday mornings to consult on a family doctor's patients. Having completed his rat studies, Charles was content with his appointment as associate professor at Case Western, where he collected blood from the rheumatologists' patients with a multitude of disorders and analyzed it in the lab to study what was occurring in patients at different stages of their illness or improvement. Without knowing how long he had, at seventy-one, neither of us wanted him to spend time finding another academic position, moving to it, and setting up a lab. He no longer treated patients.

With more freedom, we had become more active in the Northeast Ohio Mensa Society. Besides the monthly meetings, we enjoyed one particular SIG (special interest group), Mrs. Hudson's Lodgers, referring to Sherlock Holmes's landlady at 221B Baker Street. This was an undemanding version of the international Holmes society, the Baker Street Irregulars, named for the street urchins Holmes used as his eyes and ears on the street. That organization was restricted to members who passed their detailed test on the canon of Holmes stories and then were invested into the society. We also had tests on certain short stories, but they were only for fun. We had speakers, usually from academe, who specialized in the Edwardian era. Best of all, when Dwight McDonald chaired the group, we had an annual daylong meeting, with several speakers and a party in the evening to which we came dressed as a character and acted our parts. There were many good male characters, British military types, a "poulterer" (Charmaine, with her flair for costumes, dressed her husband as that), and even the Dalai Lama. Women's roles were fewer and less varied. I dressed one year as Ireney Adler, a dancer, for which I wore my tutu from a recital, although I somehow gathered from the story that Ireney was more of a nightclub dancer. Lacking any female with a better idea, they awarded me the plaque that year.

Charles had been presenting his findings at various rheumatology congresses, both locally and in Europe. In line with our plan to sightsee the area, we would usually take an added week wherever the meeting was held. For example, when he presented in Athens, we followed the meeting with a Greek Islands cruise. In this way we visited Crete and saw the Labyrinth, noted for the Minotaur myth, followed by a stop at Kuşadasi in Turkey, with an excursion to Ephesus, only one-fifth excavated after eighty years of archaeologic work at the site, and finally Patmos, with topless bathing beaches just beneath the cave where St. John wrote *Revelation*.

Reasoning that the economy was in decline and that travel would become more expensive, perhaps out of reach for the middle class, I had wanted to take the boys after they finished college to see the savannah animals of Africa. When I found a trip that extended to Central Africa to see gorillas, I signed us on. Interestingly, our group included parents and a daughter they were rewarding for completing her veterinary training. We camped in the Ngorongoro Crater and visited the Rift Valley, where the Leakeys had made their finds. Charles was able to do everything but the four-hour climb to see the mountain gorillas in Rwanda, about 80 degrees up the mountain over slippery bamboo. Meanwhile, other helpful guides took Charles to a place where gorillas often cross the road, but unfortunately not that day; however it gave Charles a chance for a prolonged conversation with locals, which he always enjoyed, as did they.

Our trip happened to take place over Christmas and New Year's, and some of our fellow travelers had chosen this schedule specifically to avoid the traditional hoopla back home. In Zaire, formerly Belgian Congo and French-speaking, where we saw lowland gorillas, two charming little girls politely asked Charles, with his white hair and beard, *"M'sieu, êtes-vous Père Noël?"* He explained that he was not, but that, it being New Year's, the time for *"cadeaux"* was past.

In 1991 the Cleveland Museum of Natural History announced a trip to a solar eclipse, to be viewed from shipboard in the Sea of Cortez. This eclipse would last a second less than seven minutes, almost as long as possible for a solar eclipse. It was special, being in the saros (family) of eclipses occurring at eighteen-year-and-several-month intervals, including the 1919 eclipse seen off the coast of Africa that demonstrated bending of light from a distant star, thus supporting Relativity Theory.

To encourage Christopher's return to a normal middle-class way of life, we invited him and met him in San Diego. To get to the ship we decided to take Amtrak's flagship, the Chief, from Chicago to San Diego. It was our idea of pleasurable train travel, with a quiz, very good food, a Vistadome, an "Indian guide" pointing out Native American ruins and casinos, and a stop in Albuquerque while they washed the train and we shopped for Native American jewelry for sale on the platform. We had worried about the train being late, and in that event would have had to fly from Albuquerque, but the Chief was right on the minute. Our fellow eclipse passengers from Cleveland who flew were delayed and almost missed the ship.

Christopher was delighted by not only the glory of this magnificent event but also the manic excitement of the viewers; he became a "shadow chaser," and subsequently went to see other eclipses. On shipboard, in the Sea of Cortez he pointed to a photograph of the Pyramid of the Sun outside Mexico City, which he remembered from my having taken him there when he was seven. We went ashore in Mazatlan, where I watched Christopher give coins to a beggar woman with a grandchild, sitting in the heavy doorframe of the church, while I was contributing to its restoration fund. (This illustrated a difference between us: Christopher is sympathetic to a need or pain that is immediate, whereas I usually try to preserve and restore for the future.) In later years we took him to eclipses in the Caribbean, the Black Sea, and Zambia.

Before returning to Cleveland, Charles and I spent a few hours at the Tar Pits of La Brea in Los Angeles, renowned for its "saber-toothed tigers" (correctly "saber-toothed cats"), which we had never visited before.

Enjoying train travel, we had long hoped to travel the Trans-Siberian Railway, second oldest national railway to France's, extending over eleven time zones from Moscow to Vladivostok. We had been told that it required a reservation eighteen months in advance, but this was difficult to plan. My friend Anne Stubblefield Morrissett had wanted to travel with us, and she suggested the Hopkins trip that she and her son Roger were taking. It included the eastern half, from Vladivostok to Irkutsk, the town in central Siberia prominent in *Doctor Zhivago*. I jumped on the idea, partly because I assumed the eastern half would take us through fields of wildflowers never exposed to fertilizers or pesticides. And that was the case.

In Irkutsk, solar physicist Aleksey Golovko showed us his observatory. Tour members more knowledgeable about solar astronomy than Charles or I were astonished at the first-class work Golovko was doing with primitive equipment.

※

We were driving out West when, having learned about the Cleveland/Lloyd Dinosaur Quarry in Utah, we decided to check it out. It was easy to track down on the correct highway. We spotted its huge multicolored beach umbrella casting the only shade for miles around. We introduced ourselves and offered to help.

"Great! I'll have somebody to talk to besides Joe here," their leader joked. They set us to work: Charles carted away wheelbarrows of already sifted sand and rubble. I sifted and brushed and sorted fossil bone from stone. I even found a fossil Allosaurus tooth. When I was handing it over, the paleontologist told me I could keep it.

Incredulous, I asked, "Don't you need it for the skeleton?"

"No, we always get more teeth than we can use. It'll be a gift from Al here."

In this way I became the proud possessor of a dinosaur tooth, which I intend to pass on to Charles Michael, who has been searching for fossils since he was three and still hopes to be a paleontologist.

Allosaurus is the state fossil of Utah.

※

Close to 300 miles southwest of Berlin is the spa town of Wiesbaden on the Rhine River. Pliny the Elder mentioned its thermal springs in his *Naturalis Historia,* and many famous people such as the German writer Johann Wolfgang von Goethe and the Russian novelist Fyodor Dostoevsky lounged in its waters to relieve various medical complaints or just to relax.

Today Wiesbaden is known as the center for the treatment of rheumatic and orthopedic diseases in Europe. It boasts several clinics staffed by internationally renowned doctors. Every year the city hosts rheumatology conferences and award ceremonies for rheumatology research. Outside of the spas is the Casino Wiesbaden, housed in a 200-year-old wine hall. From the casino comes the Carol Nachman Prize for the promotion of clinical, therapeutic, and experimental research in the field of rheumatology. Well-known scientists and researchers have won the award since it was established in the 1950s.

Charles entered his research and came in second in 1990, a prestigious recognition for his life's work.

Since Charles and I had attended half the Big Ten schools and a handful of private ones, we were on the alumni lists and received announcements of alumni trips, many environmental, some cultural. One day a brochure arrived from the University of Chicago, for a trip intending to follow in the wake of Odysseus from Troy around the eastern end of the Mediterranean all the way back to Ithaca. All of Chicago's spaces were taken, so I called the shipping line. They no longer had any of the cheap lower-deck cabins that we favored since we were always out sightseeing all day anyway, so I started to decline. Not to sail with a stateroom empty, they quickly compromised: "We'll give you a first-class cabin on the upper deck at the same price." Timothey was free to go, so I got them to put him in with the ship's doctor.

The tour assembled in Istanbul, and it became apparent that it included participants from the University of Minnesota, the

University of Chicago, and Harvard. Rumors circulated that John Updike would be in the Harvard group. "How do you make conversation with Updike?" the women asked each other.

One thing you don't say is 'I loved your books!' He's heard that many times. I think I know what I'll do," I told them.

My chance came soon. In our cabin on the top deck was an invitation for that evening to the captain's table—he didn't know we had paid the cheap rate. At a lull in the conversation I said, "Mr. Updike, you'll be interested to know why I've never read any of your books."

This got his attention, because of course I was talking about his income.

"What, what, why?"

"I lead a Great Books Discussion Group, and we read only dead authors, so you'll be happy to know you don't qualify." General laughter.

The following day we reached Troy, nine cities built each on top of the earlier, the Troy of the Trojan War being the seventh. Other sites on the tour included the cave of Polyphemus, the Cyclops, and the temple of an oracle that Odysseus had consulted for advice from ancient dead Greek heroes. We had lectures by a classicist from Harvard and an art historian from Chicago. Our day ashore in Nauplion happened to be Father's Day, giving Timothey a chance to buy his father a T-shirt featuring the Hippocratic Oath in Greek.

From Naples we were taken to the Archeological Museum in nearby Sperlonga, site of the summer villa of Tiberius, Roman emperor from 14 to 37 CE. In the museum is a collection of sculptures found in the garden of the villa. According to the curator, an unknown Greek artist commissioned by Tiberius produced them. Tiberius's cruelty and bloodlust determined his selection of the incidents from literature and mythology portrayed, including the blinding of Polyphemus. In the sculpture, Odysseus prepares to plunge a pointed pole into the one eye of the Cyclops, who is portrayed as twice the height of Odysseus. Charles, of course, observed swollen joints on the giant's hands and knobs on the rib cage. The toes of the left foot were enlarged, and so was the ankle.

Homer had composed his work 5,000 years before the statue was created and did not describe the giant Polyphemus. The sculptor depicted his model, a giant, as he was, an acromegalic individual. Acromegaly is caused by excess growth hormone and produces enlargement of the face, hands, and feet. (Of course his giant model had normal eyes, not just a single eye in his forehead, which is part of the mythology.)

When Charles drew the group's attention to what could be the earliest depiction of arthritis in a sculpture, Updike became enthusiastic and said, "Yes, Denko, write it up!" Charles did, and his paper was published in the *Journal of Rheumatology.*

⁂

One day Charles came with his typical question: "There's a meeting in Finland. Do you want to go?"

"Great! Now that we have made it to Iceland, that's the last Scandinavian country for us, and it's also close enough to Byelorussia for us to visit your cousin and her daughter, whom you've been talking about."

We included Krakow, a former capital of Poland, and a medieval city spared in World War 2 when the Russians bypassed it. We visited the Jagiellonian University, one of the oldest in Europe (1364), established by King Casimir III, who died before its completion. A few years later King Wladislaus Jagiello took up the project and put his name on it. His Queen, Jadwiga, was so enthusiastic about the university that she sold her jewels to endow a chair. She also persuaded her husband to devote his revenues (his "royalties") from the salt mine to the university, thus putting it on a stable financial basis. In the museum we were shown the book in which the university's most famous old grad, Copernicus, matriculated and the tuition paid. From Krakow we visited Oświęcim, which the Nazis called Auschwitz.

Charles's surviving cousin, Vera, and her daughter, Valery, lived in Brest, which is just over the Polish border and was the point of entry of the invading Wehrmacht in 1939. We entered Byelorussia by train from Warsaw and were held at the border for several hours in the middle of the night because we didn't catch on that they were waiting for their bribe. Finally they gave up on us as hopeless and waved us through. In Brest a park commemorated the Russians' valiant month-long stand against the Germans, with stones marking events of their resistance, including the Russian hospital from which patients in hospital garb emerged with hands in the air and were gunned down. We took Charles's relatives when we went to visit the Russian national park fifty miles north of Brest, adjoining a similar Polish park across the border, where we saw some of the last remaining European bison.

Finally we took the overnight ferry from Gdansk (Germans call it Danzig) to Helsinki. To get to Gdansk, we took the train north from Krakow and had to change in Warsaw at a ninety-second commuter stop in a suburb. Charles was using a cane but got around well enough to be carrying his small suitcase and a briefcase with slides for his upcoming talk. I had hurried ahead to get us seats on the crowded train, when to my shock I heard Charles's frightened voice yelling something I couldn't understand. I rushed to the car behind the places I had found, and there was Charles on the floor. Teenaged muggers had knocked him over, robbed him, and disembarked before the train pulled out.

Fortunately, he was not hurt. With the help of bystanders I got him up and to our seats to assess the damage, physical and financial. Those Charlie Chaplin-esque thugs had left Charles's currency of various countries and taken only his travelers' checks, which we replaced once we got to Finland.

"But Charles, what were you shouting? I could tell you were in trouble, but I couldn't make out what you were saying."

"I was crying for help in Polish."

Nicholas and Timothey both arrived by different routes at the University of Cincinnati College of Medicine. While they were in medical school, Timothey doing a cardiology fellowship, a trip was announced of a kind that offered the medical credit that Charles and I needed to keep our licenses current, a lecture in the early morning by an expert on some medical topic. In this case the tour was to Greenland (now Kalaaulit Nunaat), and the lecture series was "Medicine at the Extremes," the extremes being altitude, depths, heat, and cold. The lecturer happened to be one of our sons' professors in Cincinnati, and the timing permitted them to accompany us. We saw in the distance, looking like a small island, our first blue whale (largest animal ever to have inhabited the earth), its weight supported by water; muskoxen; an abandoned mine that was located in the oldest rock on the surface of the Earth (more than 3 billion years); and Disco Bay, where the glacier comes down at the rate of 270 feet a day(!) and calves icebergs, one of which rendezvoused with the *Titanic*. One day we went ashore at a retirement community, a big improvement over setting the elderly adrift on the ice when their days of productivity were over. As we wandered around the little park, several retired fishermen came out to investigate their guests. They tarried to demonstrate their fishing skills, and Charles, naturally, studied their hands for evidence of arthritis. The men had no idea what he was doing (our Inuit was poor) but were delighted with this attention, smiling broad toothless grins. As we reboarded our ship, Nicholas commented, "Dad, it's good you're not a urologist."

❋

With our policy of not repeating in our travels, we had no reason to return to Russia until a boat trip around Lake Baikal (the world's deepest, in central Siberia) was announced several years later. I suggested to Charles we could take the western end of the Trans-Siberian to join the group.

He had heard about a replica of an ancient Roman statue of a warrior in Moscow's Pushkin Museum. The statue came from the "true" period of art about two millennia ago, noted for detailed representation of the subject. In this case the warrior showed signs of rheumatoid arthritis, as the model must have had since it was copied so accurately but unwittingly. In line with my "travel around the edges" strategy, I scheduled an extra day for Charles to see and photograph the statue. The museum had not responded to my letter so we arrived on the wrong day (museum closed), but they let us in anyway. Charles struggled up the long flight of huge marble steps to get to the sculpture, demonstrating his enormous determination to do what was needed to achieve his ends.

I planned a second extra day in Irkutsk before the boat trip. There we arranged to be met at the hotel by Aleksey Golovko and taken to the geology museum, where we had learned on our former visit that visitors often gave specimens found in their home areas. I wanted to give them fulgurites (glass casts of tree roots produced when lightning strikes a tree in sand, transmitting heat down through the root system) and fossil crinoids (little wheel-like discs from the ancient sea in which crinoids flourished) from Berrien, my native county in south-western Michigan. They were happy with our gifts and had us make out identification cards with our names as donors.

Then we were finally ready for the tour on Lake Baikal. Victor Kuzevanov, a mathematician and botanist who ran the Irkutsk greenhouse with its collection of Siberian plants, led the excursion. Again the wildflowers were lovely. We could not see Baikal's freshwater seals in the wild because of a storm, but we saw them ashore in captivity where they were being studied.

We think of fossils as calcified bones from animals, but there are other kinds: leaf imprints, footprints, and the stromatolite Victor showed us, a fossilized colonial microorganism. I was in awe of its tremendous age, 2.1 billion years. It stood like a stone column.

Charles was experiencing increasing trouble with his bad leg. Therefore he missed the shore excursions because we had to "walk a plank" to get ashore. He didn't feel stable enough, and there was no way to help him. This trip being promoted to scientists, Charles and another elderly scientist, even more disabled, stayed onboard and chatted while the rest of us explored. I wish Charles could have seen that amazing stromatolite. He was good at appreciating everything he could do and see, and with his store of knowledge he usually saw and recognized more than most tourists, in addition to the rheumatologic connections.

That fall after our return home we tour members all received word that the weather in Siberia was so cold that Victor's greenhouse collection was in danger of losing some or all of its plants and needed both gas and electric heaters to save them. We all contributed.

⁂

In 1993 the American Chemical Society presented Charles a parchment honoring him for having been a member for fifty years.

In 1994 The Museum of Natural History announced another eclipse trip, combined with a visit to the international observatory high in the Chilean Andes. Both Charles and I were satisfied, having seen the glorious 1991 eclipse, but there were two other benefits from signing on that had nothing to do with the eclipse. They offered a pre-eclipse extension to Easter Island, and I found it hard to imagine getting there any other way. The other advantage related to Rumalon.

Charles's contact at Robapharm had died, the son and daughter of the founder weren't interested in taking over the business, and Robapharm had been sold to a French firm. By then Rumalon was available throughout the world except in the USA and Canada. Much of it was produced in Argentina, as a byproduct of their cattle industry. Our laws permit citizens to bring in medication from abroad for personal use. Often patients with incurable cancer, having exhausted all therapy available at home, are willing to grasp at straws by seeking cures elsewhere.

Because Rumalon was helping Charles's traumatic arthritis from his tipped pelvis, I left a day early for Santiago, Chile, found a pharmacy with a good supply, and bought $2,500 worth over the counter, which was a lot of Rumalon. On my return home the customs man in Miami waved me through. Charles gave Rumalon to his sister, and I gave some to Charmaine, but most of it Charles used up until his death. There is one vial left in our medicine closet.

After our group visited Easter Island with its mysterious megalithic heads, thousands of visitors converged on the eclipse from all over the world. Transportation was complicated, with little air transport and poor roads. We witnessed the eclipse in Chile high in the Andes, almost on the Bolivian border. The accommodations were simple: bunks at an army barracks while the recruits slept out on the mountain. Finally we went to the array of enormous telescopes high in the cold, clear air of the Chilean Andes.

During the final decade of the twentieth century Charles was accumulating biochemical evidence for his hypothesis about the metabolic basis of arthritis.

As the decade wore on, however, he had increasing difficulty with his bad leg. He attributed it to recurrent polio, which may have been correct, although that condition usually occurs thirty years after the original bout, whereas his had, at least, waited over eighty years, since his polio at age one. Dr. Good, his neurologist, diagnosed Parkinson's disease, although Charles showed little cogwheel rigidity, and I never saw any tremor. Timothey, an excellent clinician, had been the first to draw our attention to his father's facial rigidity, the "mask of Parkinsonism," making it difficult for Charles to project an emotional response spontaneously by smiling or laughing or replying in the usual immediate time frame. Recurrent polio and Parkinson's may have combined to produce his problems with gait. Another trait of PD is loss of control over handwriting. Charles's formerly beautiful script had deteriorated to the point where it became difficult for me to decipher.

Charles pushed himself physically, knowing that as functioning ebbed, he would never recapture it. He insisted on walking from the car to Timothey's new home, despite the ease and availability of his wheelchair, with Timothey carrying a chair for him to sit on periodically. "We walked from point A to point B," said Timothey, "catching up on life's events, and he would sit to rest." Timothey wrote about an incident that encapsulated his father's refusal to give up.

> One event can stand as an example of one of Dad's many prized qualities. Before we moved to our dream house, we lived in a smaller home ill equipped to house Mom and Dad when they visited in Pittsburgh. For one such visit I reserved a room at an elegant small hotel. The building, a registered historic landmark, functioned despite lacking an elevator.
>
> In late evening with snow and ice on the ground, Dad and I decided to use the wheelchair to navigate from the car to the front desk. When we arrived, the young night clerk quickly noticed Dad's mobility problem. The clerk was concerned about the likelihood of a fall and feared the possibility of a lawsuit. He politely informed us that since the hotel lacked an elevator we would be more comfortable down the street where accommodations were easily available. I became a bit angry at the rejection. Dad remained calm. He politely told the clerk he understood his concerns, but said, "I did not get where I am by avoiding difficult situations." Dad said he was able to navigate the stairs, thought the hotel very nice, and wished to spend the night. The clerk did not know

how to proceed, but after a few more attempts to persuade Dad otherwise, he gave in.

Dad wheeled to the bottom of the stairs. I helped
him out and he sat on the bottom step. He used his
legs and arms to push and lift himself one step at a
time. The pace was slow but steady, and we all arrived
at his room in one piece.

By this time Dad was at the peak of his profession;
he had given his alma mater a generous gift for a science wing, and could legitimately have behaved in a
haughty manner, but he did no such thing. He did not
become defensive or angry, and treated the clerk just
as he would any of his sons. The problem did not end
there; I helped Charles into the high, curtained bed.

A brochure arrived about a trip up the Orinoco River in Ven-
ezuela. One of the attractions was a stop to permit us to fly
past the world's highest waterfall, Angel Falls, named for Jimmy
Angel, the pilot who discovered it. Charles, Timothey, and I
boarded ship in Trinidad. Before casting off we were to sleep
overnight and sightsee at nine in the morning at one of two
sites: (1) a private bird sanctuary with many hummingbirds;
or (2) the Caroni Swamp, where scarlet ibises congregate and
overnight by the thousands.

I had borrowed a travel guide from the library, in which
readers were advised to visit the swamp late in the afternoon
to observe the return of the ibises after their day's foraging. I
requested the tour leader to "get a taxi and guide for the three
of us at five in the morning because the ibises, if they return in
late afternoon, fly out at dawn. When the group goes at nine,
all they will see is the trees where the ibises had overnighted."

She considered the rationale of my request and announced
that the swamp trip would leave at five. One woman said, "I
didn't come down here to get up at five." I told her, "I didn't
come down here to see all those empty trees."

In the morning we arrived at the swamp as it was getting
light, and the spectacular birds started flapping their wings
and taking off for breakfast. When we got back to the ship,
Timothey and I went to see the hummingbirds too.

I always suggested that the boys meet and eat with various tourists. That evening Charles and I were at a table with a
couple a little younger than we, and two elderly women traveling and talking together. The man introduced himself and
his wife: "We are Dr. and Mrs. Weller."

"Did you have a father or older brother at Michigan back in
the fifties who won a Nobel Prize?" Charles asked.

"Shh, shh, shh," Weller replied. "That was me, but I don't
want it to get around the ship."

"All right, we won't tell anybody," we promised.

We didn't tell Timothey until we were on the way home, but
we told him to be sure to meet Dr. Weller, and later we would
tell him something interesting about the man. Timothey talked
to Weller and even had him sign a text opposite Weller's work.

We saw the pink freshwater dolphins in the Orinoco. By
plane we saw the world's highest waterfall, Angel Falls, falling
off a tepui (a very high and narrow mesa-like structure rising
out of the jungle, with unique micro-ecology. The waterfall
was like an organdy bridal veil blown by the wind, with rain-
bows. (Since then, a claim has been made for a similar but
higher waterfall off another tepui. If this has been confirmed,
I haven't heard it.)

When Charles's leg problem made stairs more difficult, we had a stairway elevator installed.

The question was his transportation to the east side. He wanted me to drive, but the trip is forty minutes one way with no traffic at all. I told him that the time had come to use taxis. We compromised. He could tell the taxi driver where to drop him off, and, since it would be difficult for a taxi to find someone at a large university, I would pick him up.

In anticipation of a downhill course with his Parkinson's disease, we called in a contractor to convert our unused attached garage into a bedroom/sitting room/bath. Charles had commented that a certain flooring at the university was the best for him, neither too clinging nor too slippery. Our contractor tracked down that industrial flooring for Charles's new room.

While it may sound as if we did little but globetrot, the truth was that during these years Charles was working continually with the metabolic products in patients' serum and what they demonstrated about the metabolic processes of various rheumatologic ailments. Knowing that the production of growth hormone by the pituitary follows a circadian rhythm (daily low and high), he drew blood as close to 9 AM as possible, at the daily low, so that variations in its level would truly represent only changes in the arthritis, not in the daily rhythm.

I treated patients until Chuck's condition required constant care by the home health aide and myself. At the same time we sold the apartment building, and at home I worked to finish my books.

Charles W. Denko, age seventy.

CHAPTER 11

CHARLES'S FINAL YEARS (1998–2005)

SINCE NICHOLAS AND TIMOTHEY both took a hiatus after their undergraduate years, they were both in medical school during the 1990s, and had arrived, by different routes, at the same school, University of Cincinnati. By the latter years of the tenth decade Nicholas had gone to Stanford to do cancer research, and Timothey was in psychiatric residency at the University of Pittsburgh.

In 1998 Nicholas married Karen Hudson in the beautiful Stanford Chapel. The following February we invited them to join us on a trip to see the wintering monarch butterflies at the Santa Rosaria Preserve in the Trans-Volcanic Mountain Range in the state of Michoacan, Mexico.

We went by truck to see the butterflies. On their wintering mountain, billions of them hung from the trees like drapes, but not in hibernation. They have to feed and find water, and this makes for a constant river of butterflies in the air all day, down the mountain and back up. The air was full of butterflies on the wing and they were landing on people, especially those wearing red. Karen and I were constantly clicking memories with our cameras. Charles could not climb the mountain to where the butterflies hung, as he could have a few years earlier, so he stayed near the truck.

From our guide we learned of the butterfly research programs, including banding them in the United States and Canada with the hope of retrieving a minuscule fraction of the bands from wherever they rested or died en route to or in Mexico. Several years earlier Charles and I had helped with this. We had taken a day trip with the Cleveland Museum of Natural History to the Toledo area where many butterflies arrived from Canada. We swished our butterfly nets and fixed bands to the leading wing edge for identifying the place and date of the butterfly resting on its southward trip. We were told of one butterfly that flew from Toledo to Texas in five days (amazing even with the wind at its back!). Apparently that added weight from its ID did not matter to the butterfly.

We were asked to buy any bands offered by the locals so our leader could send them to the researchers. While a visitor there for a couple days had little chance of spotting a banded butterfly, the locals, including official and unofficial guides, knew the bounty offered—a dollar a tag. A local offered to sell four such bands to Nicholas and me. We bought them, and they were sent to a lepidopterist at one of the research stations gathering population figures.

❋

As the year 2000 approached, there was considerable concern about how computers would handle this, since the original programming in computers had included only the "19" but not the "20" of the century date. Many also considered it the "millennium," but since there had been no year zero, the twentieth century required 2000 to complete it.

There were special events and much excitement as 2000 drew near. We signed on for what I considered a "faux millennium" trip that circumnavigated New Zealand, with days ashore from the ship. We saw a tuatara in captivity, since the small islands between North and South Island are off limits except to researchers. These are the only living relatives of dinosaurs (except birds) and have a "third eye," a light-sensitive patch on the head that can warn of the shadow of an approaching predator bird. We saw yellow-eyed penguins, nesting wandering albatrosses, hot springs and geothermal activity, and kauri trees. They told us that these trees are older than our redwoods, and that many had been cut for sailing vessels, but this last stand had survived because it was positioned where getting them down the mountain would have been too difficult.

I especially wanted to see one of the New Zealand glowworm caves. Since the Coast Guard made our ship leave Wellington Harbor on New Year's Eve so that in the event the ship's computer crashed they would not have to come to our aid, my promised excursion to the nearby cave was impossible. Therefore I got the tour leader to taxi us back from Auckland to the Waitomo Cave to see this stunning spectacle before we left for home. The term "glowworm" is not, as I had thought, another name for fireflies. Glowworms are larval insects that attach to the cave's arch and dangle a filament like a fishing line, to catch unwitting insects for their diet. In the absolute blackness of the cave, it looks like a sky with thousands of stars, all of identical size and color.

Charles saw and enjoyed everything on this trip, but there was evidence of his decline. Before we left home I had had him count out his medication, but he had made mistakes, so I had to have the ship's doctor get him the New Zealand equivalent. We had our New Year's Eve party without a blackout.

❋

As our children were getting settled in life, Christopher was the unsettled one, but in his late twenties his sociopathy was burning out and he was becoming more attuned to a middle-class, law-abiding way of life and to the family, and he had become a "shadow-chaser." After our first unique eclipse spectacle, Charles and I had taken him to an eclipse in the Caribbean and, along with Timothey, to another in the Black Sea. By this time I was happy that he came with a request. Traveling around Central America, he had stumbled upon Docelunas (Twelve Moons), a small tropical resort hotel, abandoned, the jungle gradually swallowing it up. He had made inquiries, learned that the previous owner had lost it to drug abuse, and the bank had it on the market. Not wishing to be in the hotel business and eager to unload this asset, the bank had come down more than once on the price, from $450,000 to $270,000. Christopher asked us to come to Costa Rica to assess it and consider financing him as an hotelier. We did and could see that Docelunas certainly had possibilities.

We called a meeting. I remember the conference, with six of us around the table: Bob Gray, our accountant; Bob Higgins, our lawyer; Frank Cercone, our broker; Kirk Brady, our other broker; and Charles and me. We discussed the pros and cons as well as the unknowns, and the asking price, plus the estimated funds needed to restore the hotel. The vote was five to one against. Not even Charles, who was finally aware of Christopher's failings, agreed at first. I held out, arguing, "This is probably Christopher's last chance, and certainly the best project he has ever come up with. If it fails, the money will just come out of our estate. If it succeeds, that will be his inheritance. I say we should do it." And we did. And Christopher began to get Docelunas in working order.

When the World Explorer, the "little red ship," first of the vessels small enough to enter small bays and disembark passengers by Zodiac, was almost at the end of her usefulness but scheduled to reposition from the Mediterranean to the Amazon, a five-week trip was announced. It described a huge letter "J," following the mid-Atlantic Ridge from island to island, from the Canaries down to Tristan da Cunha, then proceeding westward to South Georgia and finally to the Falklands. The crossing took five weeks, with many days entirely at sea, which attracted passengers like us who relished lectures, time on deck, and interesting fellow travelers. By my "travel around the edges" strategy, I started us out two days early, giving us an extra day in Madrid to see the Spanish art in the Prado Museum and a second day to get to the island of Gomera in the Canaries to hear from the waiters at our lunch venue their "whistling language," which consisted of words placed on a whistle, which could carry from one mountaintop to another.

On Tenerife, where the tour originated, we met our fellow passengers, some of whom had been delayed by bad flying weather over the Atlantic. (Delays like this are another good reason to set out early.) The stops included the Canaries; the Cape Verde Islands, pivotal in the slave trade; Ascension, where American pilots refueled in World War 2 and the mantra was "If we miss Ascension, my wife gets a pension"; St. Helena, where Napoleon spent his terminal exile; Tristan da Cunha; South Georgia (geographically part of Antarctica), with thousands of king penguins and a few nesting albatrosses, whose chicks spend an entire year on the nest exercising their wings before their first make-or-break flight; and the Falklands, with, years after the war, fenced-off live minefields.

Charles, a stamp collector, wrote:

Tristan da Cunha was the farthest from other human habitations of any settlement on earth. Under the protection of England, it had only connections by sea, no landing strip at that time. It was of interest to philatelists, and stamps were one of their two main industries, fishing the other.

Tristan had a rheumatologic ailment of interest to Charles. He talked to the British consul and examined several of the residents. Charles wrote:

We found it to have a unique rheumatologic problem. The footpaths are narrow and rocky. Cattle roam free until they are needed for meat, at which time they are slaughtered on the mountainsides. After butchering them, the young men carry the quarters down the steep hillsides, bracing their footsteps so as not to fall, until reaching the small settlement.

Many young men developed severe lumbosacral pain, difficult to control despite use of pain-relieving medication prescribed by the island physician, along with physiotherapeutic measures. This back pain and stiffness created a serious problem requiring a diagnosis. The nearest specialist for referral was several hundred miles away, in the country of South Africa. By the time patients reached South Africa, the sea trip and rest had provided relief. X-ray and blood studies relieved the island doctor's worst worries about joint-destroying arthritis. When the consulting physician learned that these men were accustomed to carry on their shoulders a quarter of an ox down steep mountain paths, or half a wild sheep, which might weigh 300 pounds, the prescription was clear: cut up the meat before starting down the mountain. The results confirmed the analysis. Denouement: When I saw these men some months after their new program was in place, they had a normal range of motion with normal muscle power and no joint tenderness. They returned to carrying meat (in smaller pieces) with no recurrence of symptoms.

❋

Although not a new century, 2000 ushered in a new aspect of our lives. Our children had come late because of my obstetrical problems. Our sons were late in marrying because of professional education. On Valentine's Day, 2000, when Charles was already eighty-three, we welcomed our first grandchild, Kristina Joanna, daughter of Timothey and Lisa Claire Thomas. That relationship did not last, and in August of 2000 Timothey married Patricia Arlene Venditto in the garden of the Morning Glory B&B that had served as a station for the pre-Civil War Underground Railroad. Their daughter, Madeleine Grace, was born May 9, 2001, joined on November 26, 2003 by their son Charles Michael.

Nicholas and Karen's older son, Louis Alexandar, was born June 11, 2001, in Kramatorsk, Ukraine, and adopted that December. (Charles lived long enough to see these four grandchildren.) They were followed by Nicholas and Karen's second son, Jackson Gilberto, born September 3, 2006 in Guatemala and adopted in the winter of 2008, following legal problems regarding adoptions in Guatemala, and by Christopher and Diane Maria Bedoya Ruiz's daughter, Emily Rose, born March 10, 2011 in Costa Rica, where Christopher and Diane had married and by this time Christopher had his resort hotel, Doce-lunas, up and running.

Thus our lives became recomplicated. We visited Kristina every few months in Archbald, a small town near Scranton, Pennsylvania. While Timothey, Patricia, and their family were more accessible in Pittsburgh, Nicholas and Karen and Louis were 2,000 miles away, in Menlo Park, then Woodside, near Palo Alto, California. Charles and I were present the day of the birth of each of the three born in this country. The adoption people suggested that we should give little Louis time to make some of the necessary adjustments to parents and a new home before introducing him to grandparents; thereafter Charles and I visited the California branch of the family at least yearly.

❋

As early as the mid-1990s Charles began to complain occasionally about his left leg. "Complain" is too strong a word. He was never a complainer. In medicine, however, we talk about the "chief complaint." He occasionally "mentioned" that his leg damaged by polio was giving him trouble, i.e., by being weak. He drew my attention to how cold it was, and hard to keep warm despite wearing a sock to bed. He attributed it to recurrent polio. His gait became affected, and Dr. Good attributed it to his Parkinson's disease. Perhaps he had both. Therefore when we traveled, it was helpful to have one of our sons along, particularly for boarding and disembarking. The boys joked that their parents traveled with their own porters.

The stairs became too hard for Charles. Fortunately we had had a stairway elevator installed in anticipation of need. We also had the unused, attached garage converted into a bedroom/sitting room/bath with just three steps down, so he could avoid a flight of stairs altogether. Ken Spiro, our builder, tracked down special commercial flooring used at the university that Charles had found just right, neither slippery nor clinging. Dr. Good had diagnosed Charles's Parkinson's disease when he showed few of the classic signs, mainly more difficulty walking. From a cane he went to a walker, and later to a wheelchair.

As we entered the twenty-first century Charles was able to accomplish his last two challenging trips with little difficulty from his Parkinson's disease.

A trip was announced for an eclipse to be seen in Zambia on the summer solstice in June 2001. We were beginning to use eclipses (in the Caribbean and in the Black Sea) as a good way to spend time with Christopher, since he seemed never to tire of that experience, almost like an epiphany. So we invited Christopher and also Nicholas's wife, Karen, as a chance for her to see savannah animals. Our group of four worked well because Christopher roomed with his father and helped him with luggage and on and off transportation. Karen and I shared a room. In line with my "travel around the edges" policy, we started a day and a half early. The first half day was planned to arrive in Atlanta early and taxi out to Stone Mountain, the Civil War Memorial honoring the Confederacy, the work of Gutzon Borglum, better known for Mount Rushmore with the four presidents, which he designed but did not live to complete. It had seemed to me that one should not go through Johannesburg, where our tour began, without visiting Soweto

(Southwest Township), where apartheid took its first hit, the beginning of the end. We rented a taxi for our extra day prior to the tour and saw the homes of Archbishop Desmond Tutu and Nelson Mandela. (The guide noted with pride that this was the only street in the world with the homes of two Nobel laureates.) We also saw their enormous hospital, where many medical students from Europe and America volunteer to work (and learn) during their free quarters. We happened to be in South Africa on the twenty-fifth anniversary of the first victory against apartheid, celebrated by a huge youth rally. While the three of us returned to the hotel, Christopher went to the rally and reported that he was one of just a handful of white young men, and the event was peaceful and respectful.

Joining our tour group, we went first to Mala Mala, a private wildlife-viewing facility just outside Africa's first national park, Krueger. (This was chosen because in Krueger you had to drive your own car, whereas at Mala Mala, they had Land Rovers and guides for visitors.) We saw the usual assortment of animals, but in addition, the one I particularly wanted to see put in an appearance, to my delight: a pangolin, a mammal with scales that rolls up into a ball for protection. We then headed to Zaire for the eclipse, then north to Victoria Falls. Finally we rode part of the distance back to Johannesburg via the renowned Edwardian "Blue Train," Rovos Rail, with mahogany paneling and brass fittings. It was a reflection of past gracious living, but we traveled through Zimbabwe, the southern part of the former Rhodesia, which had in those days exported grain to other parts of the world. By the time of our trip the dictator Robert Mugabe had already trashed Zimbabwe.

With Christopher's help, Charles made it home without incident.

That same year, Charles showed me a brochure about a trip through the Northwest Passage in late summer by the Russian icebreaker *Kapitan Klebnikov,* and wanted to go. We flew to Resolute, Nunavut, in the Canadian Arctic. The captain and the ship's doctor came to our cabin after we boarded the ship and advised Charles against the trip, but he persuaded them he could manage—and did. He had only one small accident, which could have happened to anyone. Thrown off his seat in rough waters, Charles struck his head on a locker and required several stitches in his scalp. As long as the ocean was ice-covered, as it was between the islands, the passage was very smooth. For meals, by mutual understanding the passengers left places nearest the entry to the dining room for us.

Charles enjoyed the magnetic North Pole, where the compass went wild. We went ashore at Beechey Island where Rear Admiral Sir John Franklin's ill-fated expedition had wintered in the mid-nineteenth century during his voyage to map a section of the Northwest Passage. Their demise was assured because they would not accept the help of the "ignorant savages" who brewed tea of pine needles to counteract scurvy. Polar bears and their cubs wandered on the ice; walruses sprawled in piles on ice floes and peeled off at our approach. Ashore were Arctic hares, foxes, and a great number of geese.

They disembarked us by Zodiac and helicopter. They made special helicopter trips for Charles, since the pitted ground of the rough tundra could have given him a broken leg, so he could see the animals and snow geese. He was captivated by the muskoxen, attributing to them social conscience when he saw the protective ring they formed around their juveniles at the frightening sound of the helicopter. U.S. Coast Guard regulations did not allow our ship to enter American ports because the *Klebnikov* lacked cough shields over the buffet service, so we went ashore by Zodiac in northern Alaska.

The trip was planned to disembark in Providenya, Northeast Russia, the terminus of the Northwest Passage, just beyond the Bering Strait, in September 2001.

We were in Russian waters near the end of our trip on September 11 when hijacked airplanes ran into the Twin Towers in New York and the Pentagon in Virginia, and crashed in Shanksville, Pennsylvania, in a plane whose intelligent and socially conscious passengers made sure that only they were killed, no one on the ground. The ship's PA announced in the early morning that word had been received of a catastrophe in the USA. We were invited up to the radio room for the report. With only the words to go by, we never felt the same impact as those who watched transfixed all day, over and over, the crumbling Twin Towers.

We arrived in Providenya to learn that the U.S. was not allowing any flights in or out. This gave us an extra five days in the far northeast part of Russia. We went to an ancient Inuit anthropologic dig from 700 years earlier, and an island with two breeds of Pacific puffins nesting in enormous numbers. We visited the school at an Inuit village, where portraits of Tolstoy, Dostoevsky, and other Russian writers graced the walls.

Finally a flight was permitted to Nome, Alaska, where we made connections to Anchorage and home via Salt Lake City.

❊

Over the years we had visited Charles's brother, John, and his first wife, Gloria, and family in Chicago, Seattle, and Amarillo, and later John and his second wife, Susan, in Rancho Santa Fe, California. I always admired John for the fact that he did not stop learning after his active schooling, and was a host willing to share the novelties of his region. His interests were varied and wide. In the desert country around Amarillo, he went looking for and took us to seek fossils of Western Hemisphere camels that had become extinct. He served on the board of the Amarillo Symphony. After his retirement, in California he and Susan took us to see a century plant in bloom and a rare kind of tree, the Torrey pine, in a state park that preserved it. He was a skilled and avid photographer and sent us copies of pictures he took when the family gathered for a visit or event, such as Bobby and Togi's wedding, at which our two little boys had been attendants. Nicholas and Timothey had inadvertently donned each other's jackets, but we didn't realize it until we saw the pictures, with Nicholas's sleeves halfway up his forearms, Timothey's down over his hands.

It was lovely of John and Susan to invite Charles out to California, along with Timothey, Patricia, and infant Madeleine, to take good care of him and keep him comfortable and happy, while giving me a little respite.

Sadly, two years later John preceded Charles in death as a result of having omitted an advised colonoscopy when he was in good health. When we learned of John's malignancy, Charles and I went out to see him once more, and I let them have final brother-to-brother time alone. On that trip, in the clear air and at an altitude, I finally saw the phenomenon I had heard and read about but never witnessed: the stars actually twinkled.

※

Geneva's chemistry graduates were invited for a reunion, where they were given an opportunity to tell their experiences. I told Charles that he was no longer thinking fast enough to speak extemporaneously, so I advised him to write out his remarks.

He did not heed my advice, tried to speak off the cuff, and the results were considerably below his erstwhile fluency. It was his last such attempt.

Charles's driving was showing problems. I don't recall the reason for the first accident, but the second resulted from a problem with depth perception. He ran into a parked car, rolled his Volvo over, and the police found him unhurt, hanging by the seatbelt. The only thing that suffered damage (besides the car) was his beautiful sports jacket, which they had to cut off to make sure he wasn't bleeding. Charles didn't utter a syllable when I took his keys. Christopher said I should have taken them sooner, and he was right. I had become our only driver, somewhat inconvenient for me, immensely so for him.

We worked out a plan whereby Charles took a taxi to the university and I picked him up at the rheumatology office. In fact he soon cut back to half days, and then to just one such a week. Then his colleague and friend, Charles Malemud, began coming to the house Wednesday mornings to help get his data ready for publication rather than lose them. (Malemud told me that he had never seen such meticulous record keeping in data books. I had seen the books, of course, but I thought every scientist kept them that way.) Charles was grateful for Malemud's help, as was I. In fact Charles Malemud, after many efforts, has finally (January 2016) found a British journal (*Archives of Medicine*) happy to publish Charles's last unpublished paper, with historical additions and editorial corrections under our three names: Denko, Denko, and Malemud. At the interface between art and medicine, it is the paper about that engraving on that two-and-a-half-millennia-old Scythian gold vessel that we saw at the Hermitage Museum in St. Petersburg, portraying a shaman examining a patient with inflammatory arthritis, who is wincing with pain.

Charles had two short hospitalizations, one after a fall and another with a bladder infection. Although the hospitalization was necessary, the attendants did not get him out of bed as ordered and his mobility suffered. He was sent to a nursing home for very beneficial physical therapy with his walker before returning home. One activity the home offered was word games, so I made sure they took him to that, but his deterioration was illustrated when he complained, "I was the best one in the class, but still they won't let me go home."

When our friend Gerry Thorrat (longtime member of Great Books and a lupus patient of Charles's) learned that the *Cleveland Jewish News* was collecting Holocaust material, she linked Cynthia Dettelbach (their editor for thirty years) and Charles for a telephone interview. In her article she commented on how this sensitive Gentile gave way to tears over the memory, sixty years after finding Jewish orphans' relatives.

As the Parkinson's disease worked its inexorable course, Charles struggled to finish his life's work with the help of Dr. Charles Malemud, former student, colleague, and friend. As a young scientist Dr. Malemud had visited Charles's lab and recognized the importance of his work sooner than other rheumatologists. Dr. Malemud generously contributed time and effort to get Charles's latest research data ready for publication.

When Charles was no longer able to drive and then had gradually cut back his work hours, Dr. Malemud began coming to our house one morning a week to accomplish this final task. They would sit in the renovated garage, and after the day's work, discuss national and world politics, the situation in Israel, history, art, and other subjects of mutual interest to these intelligent and intellectual men, as both Charleses loved to do. As Charles pointed out, Russians are great talkers, usually around a samovar. I should have thought to get ours out for them.

*

In the spring of 2003 Charles received an invitation from Penn State to a weekend planned to honor graduates who had received their Ph.D.s fifty and more years earlier. Family members were welcome. I couldn't reach Christopher; Timothey would attend with his family directly from Pittsburgh; Nicholas was scheduled to be at a meeting in Denver. At least that was closer than California, and Nicholas arranged to detour to Pennsylvania for his father's recognition. Charles was able to travel, but getting him to central Pennsylvania posed a problem. I needed help with transportation for him to and from Penn State.

I asked Father John at St. Herman's House of Hospitality, which our church had supported over the years, but he told me that his vows forbade his touching another man. (I thought they often helped the sick.) After a week of fruitless efforts, I finally got Charles to State College by myself and into the Nittany Lion Hotel. Nicholas and Timothey and his family arrived as planned and helped with their father.

The ceremony was simple but impressive. On the wall was a modern recognition arrangement that looks like a branching tree, with each honoree and his data engraved on one of the metal leaves. When Charles' name was called first as the longest-time Ph.D. in attendance, having graduated sixty-three years prior, I rolled him up to the platform.

Other events were standard, a luncheon and exhibition of research work, but the best part was a trip with Nicholas and

Timothey, Patricia, Madeleine, and little Charles Michael to the Milk Pail, where the rich milk of Penn State's College of Agricultural Sciences is sold as ice cream. Over the years, whenever Charles and I have driven through that part of Pennsylvania, we have always stopped for ice cream. (Timothey remembered a funny habit of Charles's. Not to be the one asking for something when I was trying to keep down his weight, he would often say, e.g., "The boys want some ice cream.")

❋

In early 2003, we sold the Parkview, I gave up practice (I did not renew my license), and worked to finish several books I was writing. I began employing home health aides. The agency I used had a number of professional men, not citizens, and therefore unable to pursue their careers because of lack of a license in this country. For short periods we had a dentist and a gastroenterologist. Then we had Jonas Jasaitis, with degrees in sociology and pedagogy in Lithuania. He worked with Charles until the political situation stabilized and made it feasible to return home. Then we were fortunate to get our final home health aide, Valerij Onipko, a Ukranian-trained physician who had practiced in Europe first as a family physician, then as a forensic pathologist. He was a naturalized citizen who had brought his family here for opportunities, but he did not have a medical license here. He brought a wealth of practical ideas and help for Charles in decline. Better yet, even though he had never known Charles in his prime, he loved him like an uncle. He promised to stay as long as we needed him before finding work better suited to his medical training and expertise, which he did. When Charles slept, Val worked on an MBA by distance learning from the University of Colorado in Boulder. He has subsequently worked for pharmaceutical companies overseeing multisite research projects, an excellent use for a person of his training and abilities.

As the Parkinson's disease worked its inexorable course, Charles struggled to finish his life's work with the help of Charles Malemud, his colleague, former student, and friend.

※

As Charles went into decline, our sons visited whenever possible. Nicholas, in California, served on grant review boards at NIH (National Institutes of Health) in Bethesda, Maryland. He explained the situation to the general in the army (who dispersed travel money), and he kindly arranged a stopover in Cleveland for Nicholas. Timothey would often bring the children on Saturday afternoon, and then take them to the beach. Christopher came whenever his hotel required a trip to Washington.

Val helped make Charles's final years as good as possible. He and I took Charles many places, such as to the Cleveland Astronomical Society dinner meetings, where I introduced him as Charles's nephew, to make him more comfortable with his menial role for a highly educated person. Everyone warmed to this intelligent, reserved gentleman and commented on how fortunate we were to have him.

Val could move Charles from the wheelchair to the car. We took Charles to the nearby Cuyahoga National Park where from a parking area we were able to watch the great blue heronry, where male birds were bringing in twigs to refurbish the fifty or more of last year's nests in preparation for the return of the females.

We took Charles to Caesar's Creek, a water conservancy project of the Corps of Engineers, which lets visitors register for a permit to prospect for fossil trilobites. We were unsuccessful.

We visited a Russian Orthodox monastery in the hills of upstate New York, where Val and his wife had already purchased a lot in the cemetery. The monks were kind to Charles, as Val had promised. They invited the entire congregation to dinner, and during the otherwise silent meal, one monk read aloud in Russian about the lives of saints. We returned from New York to find a tick on Charles's leg with a "target" of inflammation, but tests showed he did not have Lyme disease.

Val helped me take Charles, who always enjoyed train travel, in Amtrak's special accommodations for the handicapped, to Palo Alto, California, to visit Nicholas, Karen, and little Louis. I made sure that Val had a day trip around San Francisco. As we flew home, Charles said, "I want to go again." I agreed, "If you're well enough next year." But it was not to be.

In 2004 Val and I flew Charles to Costa Rica to see the newly opened DoceLunas, Christopher's small, charming tropical resort hotel at Jaco on the Pacific Ocean. I was happy to see the good taste Christopher showed in furnishing the hotel with handcrafted furniture by local woodworkers and art by local artists.

Jaco is a surfers' paradise, where Val and I bodysurfed. We went to see crocodiles in the river. A friend of Christopher's took us to the nearby national park where we saw a three-toed sloth, which was hanging slothfully from a tree branch. We saw capuchin monkeys and a brown basilisk, nicknamed a "Jesus Christ lizard," running on the water without breaking the surface tension.

At breakfast, Charles spilled some syrup as he ate French toast. "This'll determine whether I get another trip," he said.

"Your travel doesn't hinge on fine motor coordination. We don't care if you spill a little syrup. Christopher has plenty of help to clean it up."

But Charles did not get too much out of this trip.

"How did you hear about this place?" he asked.

I was happy to see what good taste and judgment Christopher showed with Docelunas. Later it was listed as the eleventh best (non-chain) hotel in Central America. In 2014 Fodor named it their "Hotel of the Year" in Central America.

One day back home Charles asked me, "Who is running this establishment?"

I replied, "This establishment is your home, and I am running it."

It is a terrible thing to see the once fine mind of someone you love come to this.

❋

When Charles realized he was approaching his big deadline, one remark of his almost broke my heart: "I haven't done enough. I should have accomplished more."

"No, you've done marvelously, as a family man and as a scientist."

Dr. Malemud affirmed that the ideas Charles was working with are important to our understanding of arthritis. He wrote summaries of Charles's achievements for his long biography. Both Dr. Malemud and I were happy to learn that four research groups around the country are carrying Charles's work forward.

Charles and other achievers, as they approach life's end, are likely to have the same feeling as did Dr. Samuel Johnson, eighteenth-century English lexicographer, writer, and critic, and compiler of the first English dictionary: "It is a most mortifying reflexion for any man to consider, *what he had done,* compared with *what he might have done.*" In the case of Charles, I reminded him how his life as a family man—Indian Guides, Boy Scouts with the boys, shopping and cooking on weekends, time spent with me, traveling beyond conferences—reduced what he might have done as a scientist, but that wherever he was, he was always observing and thinking about arthritis. Given that time and energy are limited, his choices were good, his life was rich, and he was blessed with abundant energy and an eighty-nine-year life span.

⁂

During the weekend of October 15–16, 2005, all three sons came home for different reasons, such as class reunions. On the morning of October 18, I entered Charles's room and found him with face blue and without respiration or pulse. I administered mouth-to-mouth respiration, thumped his chest rhythmically, and was able to restart breathing and heartbeat, but he remained unconscious. The Emergency Medical Services arrived within five minutes, asked how to code him (*"Save him!"*), but lost his pulse and respiration on the drive to the hospital.

I had planned the funeral in advance and had gathered material for his obituary. On the memorial card given to visitors attending the funeral were these words from Ralph Waldo Emerson:

> To laugh often and much; to win the respect of intelligent people and the affection of children; to earn the appreciation of honest critics and endure the betrayal of false friends; to appreciate beauty; to find the best in others; to leave the world a bit better whether by a healthy child, a garden patch, or a redeemed social condition; to know even one life has breathed easier because you lived. This is to have succeeded.

His sons returned for Russian Orthodox funeral services by Father Yves Babbich at the McGreevey Funeral Home in Lakewood on October 21, and Charles was buried the following day in the Locust Grove Cemetery in his hometown of Ellwood City, on a hillside overlooking the hills of western Pennsylvania. A soldier played taps. Four-year-old Madeleine laid a yellow rose on his casket. On his side of the green granite grave marker, I placed a benzene ring for physiologic chemistry and a caduceus for medicine.

*"The first time I ever heard about __________ was in a
lecture of Denko's about twenty-five years ago."*

— A frequent comment by his former students and his colleagues

*"If I had avoided difficult situations
I wouldn't be where I am today."*

—Charles W. Denko

Tribute to Charles Denko.

I first met Chuck many years ago on the occasion
of his marriage to Joanne. Whenever I hear *Some
Enchanted Evening,* I recall that happy event.

Chuck has made an indelible impact on my life.
Later, unable to walk steadily, he slowly mounted the
thirteen steps up to the top of our summer home.
"What a magnificent view of the lake!" he exclaimed. I
watched him descend the same way — a step at a time
on his backside. He has helped me understand the
power of an indomitable will.

Now, as I approach ninety years, I think of Chuck
as I climb the thirteen steps. The hardest steps are not
always climbed with our feet.

Thanks, Chuck.
Blaise Levai, B.D., M.Div., Ed.D.

[I greatly appreciated Blaise's glowing tribute. However, I was
taken aback by his astonishment, no doubt resulting from
the long interval of Charles's decline when our paths did not
cross and Blaise had no way to witness Charles's adaptations
to his diminishing strength. Living with Charles, I was not at
all surprised by his use of his arms to supplement his legs, just
as he had done at the historic registry hotel. — *Joanne Denko*]

CHAPTER 12

CHARLES'S HUMANITY

WHAT IS USUALLY CONSIDERED a pleasant personality Charles had in spades. He found it easy to make first contact with new acquaintances, particularly women. He almost always inquired where they "came from" or "grew up", and usually responded from his remarkable knowledge of not only our country but Europe as well, to inquire or comment and show interest in the other's background. This talent, I soon realized, resulted from the fact that in the years between Charles's and my growing up, the curriculum had changed to reduce "geography" from an ongoing exposure from elementary school through high school and including college to the four years from fourth through seventh grades that I had.* His fund of

---

* A recent article in the *Cleveland Plain Dealer* deplores the current lack of geographic knowledge in our people. This is partly why we are fast losing our beliefs in our exceptionalism, especially in the natural marvels in our country. The author indicated that in retirement he is completing his fourth grade education (in geography) by visiting all the places in our country that he has missed.

knowledge was augmented by his discipline of reading *Time* magazine from cover to cover weekly to be informed on current events domestic and foreign, for, among other things, his participation in Lincoln-Douglas debates. (His team beat Harvard one year). I adopted his method but preferred, by then, *Newsweek*. Editorially I might comment that these interests/ habits kept him educated through life in a way that few were then or are now.

Another interest of his consisted of languages. This began with the fact that he grew up in a community settled largely by eastern European immigrants. His father, whom he loved and admired, could quickly pick up by ear enough to get by with someone speaking a related language. Charles had or developed this ability. For fun Iza, my medical school friend, and Charles would sometimes converse, he speaking Russian and Iza Polish, each perfectly understanding the other. (The spoken languages are almost identical, but Polish uses the Roman alphabet, Russian the Cyrillic.) Often, in a new country, Charles would begin by inquiring of our taxi driver some of the common phrases in the new language. Only once, in the Pyrenees, did Charles come up completely at a loss when someone spoke to him in Euskara, the major Basque language.

From general reading he picked up information on other unrelated languages. While he was treating rheumatologic patients, sometimes he would have elderly women who had come north from the South Carolina and Georgia coast or offshore islands. He would inquire from them about the slave language, Gullah, which had evolved from an African language or languages often mixed with plantation English. They would be not only surprised but delighted by his interest and would enjoy teaching him about that language.

He enjoyed learning about other cultures. One way to do

this was possible when we had bilingual guides for days at a time. We all regretted that he could not attempt the steep four-hour climb to visit the mountain gorillas in Rwanda, but he enjoyed spending a day with the locals, who told about their efforts to support a family and educate their younger siblings.

I observed that women seemed particularly drawn to Charles. I think this was partly because he so often offered to help, and women were the ones in need of help, usually putting the finishing touches on food preparation. They appreciated his low-key company.

Finally, unlike most "war stories," his were not of a combat nature, but very interesting anecdotes of his nutrition studies on conscientious objectors, his keeping the identifiable penicillin vials out of the hands of the cruel black marketeers, and his relocating Jewish orphans with their family members.

Charles's relationship with men was more distant, partly because as a non-drinker and a devoted family man, he did not go to the pub after work on Fridays or play golf with other physicians. Although he could easily walk the eighteen holes and was a pretty good duffer, he preferred to spend his free time at home with us. He enjoyed gardening and playing with the boys. He did not indulge in the usual male banter, although he could respond to male talk about cars and how all the sports teams were faring. Also, at a time when most physicians were men, he was not in the group that referred patients back and forth, since he was usually the end of the referral chain. He always considered himself primarily a biochemist, applying his biochemical base to the treatment of patients. I think they would have liked him better if he had been a hail-fellow-well-met.

As I said, in many ways he was a family man par excellence. Early in our marriage, he taught me to write scientific papers and did everything else he could to help with any of my projects. During the two years I was at "bed rest" carrying our children, he did everything possible to help me get through that difficult, worrisome and monotonous period. Although he was a romantic, producing a red rose on our "monthiversary," he was primarily a man of deeds, not words. He did not indulge in flattery, cajolery, or palaver about love. He saved and invested for the futures of all of us, including the boys' education. He did the "boy things" with them. Originally intending to use his international congresses as a way for me to travel with him, we later included the boys when appropriate, as well as for "travel without slides" to such places as Alaska, Mesa Verde, Prince Edward Island, Greenland, the eastern end of the Mediterranean (following in the wake of Odysseus), and short trips around Australia during the sabbatical. He himself liked high latitudes, including not only Russia but the Arctic and Antarctic.

Twenty-five years into our marriage, circumstances brought out Charles's one fatal flaw. This unfortunately evidenced itself in the family. He would not or could not discipline a child whose behavior cried out for it. When one son's misbehavior was slipping down to delinquency, without help from Charles I had to try to discipline, argue, explain to the judge (I made one mistake: to be fair I included Christopher's assets and strengths), plead for intensive treatment in a residential setting to turn him around—without success. I credit Charles with keeping in touch with him when I said that either Christopher or I with the younger ones had to leave the house. After many years Christopher gradually returned to a normal middle-class way of life. When another son displayed a different problem, Charles had learned. I credit him with cooperating with me immediately, enabling us to get that boy turned around in much shorter time.

Charles was also interested in the arts. He was not feigning interest to impress me. He told about how his sister Helen complained that he would not let her play popular music on their new radio on Saturday afternoon because he wanted to hear the Metropolitan Opera. He also had made friends with an older woman artist, who painted his portrait to take home to his mother, and who advised him to buy a certain museum-quality black silk and silver Caucasian belt, and to give it to his future bride, which he did.

Another interest of Charles's, one that I did not share, was cooking. He learned ethnic cooking from his sister Munya and taught the boys to make *blinyi* ("skinny pancakes"), borsch, and beef à la Stroganoff. He also took them out to lay in supplies. He prepared our weekend meals, but the ones he enjoyed more were our dinners for guests, with his Russian specialties. In a time when physicians treated each other for "professional courtesy," after each birth we had the obstetrician and his wife over for dinner and the evening.

Charles was twice voted the most humorous man in the class, in high school and again in college. His humor was never sarcastic or hurtful. On his desk were two mottoes: "Avoid obfuscation," a funny way to connote "Be clear," and "A cluttered desk is the sign of an ordered mind." I don't know whether it is the sign, but he certainly had both.

About his personality, my friend Iza summed it up: "He was smart, friendly, easy to be with."

❈

Charles was sensitive, both to his own pain and to the pain of others. In fact, before we as a society began to recognize that men should get in touch with their soft inner feelings, Charles was able to cry. The very first time he took me to visit his family, Chipper, his young nephew's dog, had just fifteen minutes earlier been killed by a car, and Charles cried with little Bobby. When interviewed by the *Cleveland Jewish News* about his postwar work in locating family members with whom to place Jewish orphans, he cried—sixty years after the fact. And when he finally could no longer deny his son's delinquency, he sat on the bed and sobbed.

He was a man who, as soon as he knew what he wanted, was willing to wait and work for it, as for example, the evening at the mixer when he decided that I was the one he wanted to marry—and courted me for almost three years, giving me time to grow up and get within shouting distance of my goal to be a medical doctor. On the other hand, when an opportunity presented itself, he was ready to snatch it, as with the chance to take his professor's advice to get his own M.D., which he did when the G.I. Bill became available, and he attended medical school. However he did not avail himself of opportunities that would divert him from his goal of human biochemistry. When offered a place on the prestigious Manhattan Project (working on the atomic and nuclear bombs), he explained that it was the wrong kind of chemistry for his interests and training. He also had taken his father's advice to save out of every paycheck, with the result of having money available for travel, investments, education, and the three homes we bought.

Another beautiful trait of Charles's, a trait he shared with his father, was his willingness and wish for others to have things that he could not have himself. Charles had no problem with the rest of us getting to the few places too difficult for him. His father, who had hoped to attend night school in America, had helped both sons pay college fees and offered to help his daughters as well. He even offered to borrow money against his pension to get me through medical school if my father had not come around about our marriage. Having collected material and written a book on envy, I saw no evidence of it in father or son.

*

From his earliest years Charles's predominant character trait was determination. When he decided what he wanted, he pursued it wholeheartedly.

An early display of determination came at age eight when, without his mother and far from home in a different state, young Charles spent five months working to strengthen his damaged leg after surgery, with the help of the physical therapist at the Shriners' Hospital. When a patient does not cooperate in his own therapy, the system cannot afford to continue expending expertise and time and money working with him. In days long before Ronald McDonald, Charles would have been sent home to his family. Instead, as long as he continued to improve, they worked to give him back all the strength possible to his damaged leg. I did not think to ask, but I suspect that as a child he may have fantasized accomplishing a perfect leg. It must have been years before he realized the quantum difference between his polio-damaged leg and his imperfect, "gimpy leg" as he called it, that was good enough for him to live the exceptional life of an adult scientist.

With his giftedness, the additional assignments his caring first grade teacher gave him to bring him up to speed in English did not require special determination to accomplish. His parents, too, unlike many then and now, were happy to accept any additional help offered to their children. (Jim Walker, a French teacher, member of our Great Books Discussion Group, told me of the angry mother who came to complain when he gave her talented daughter extra work in French!)

Whenever Charles recognized his need for help or guidance, he was more than willing to seek and accept it. When
he won the competitive scholarship for his county, he did not
choose a school some friend was attending (as many do these
days). He went straight to his chemistry teacher for advice in
deciding where to use it, since this man was the only person
he knew who was familiar with the system of higher education
in which he could move toward his goal of becoming a chemist. That teacher directed him to Geneva, a liberal arts college
near home that had already been recognized for the high quality of its education in chemistry. Under the influence of A. K.
Anderson, Ph.D., at Penn State, he narrowed down his hopes
for chemistry to biochemistry, rheumatology in particular,
since his respected professor was already wheelchair-bound
with rheumatoid arthritis, for which there was little help then
beyond aspirin and gold compounds, which produced problems of toxicity.

After medical school and internship, Charles pursued a residency in internal medicine (necessary to enter a specialty). There
he met Del Bergenstahl, a friend of his younger brother John's,
who, at the University of Chicago where much of the preliminary
work toward the atomic bomb was accomplished, had access
to radioisotopes, which had become available and useful for
medical research. From Del he learned how to study cartilage
in rats with radioactive sulfur. This gave him the maximum
preparation to study the biochemistry of arthritic disorders.

A parallel aspect of Charles's life that demonstrated his determination, along with willingness to wait and work toward his
goal, was his patience in delaying marriage until I was ready.
Then Charles did all he could to get me through the total of two
years of difficult "bed rest" to deliver our three sons, because
of all my obstetrical problems.

Thus Charles was future-oriented and given to planning, just the opposite of impulsive or given to instant gratification. Yet he was quick in an emergency, as when he pulled three-year-old Timothey by the hair out of Moll's pool.

To be ready for opportunities, Charles had taken his father's advice, to save from the first paycheck. When he was in the post-World War 2 Occupation of Europe, this was easy, because Europe was flat and there was little to buy. Furthermore, all his needs were covered by the service and he had never indulged in the two most expensive extravagances, burning money (smoking) and metabolizing it (drinking). The commanding officers urged the men to buy war bonds, and these became his nest egg for later needs. However he realized that saving by itself was not enough. The savings needed to be invested, to work until needed. Therefore he and his friend taught themselves investment principles, which were so successful that twice he was offered work at brokerages. But of course his heart was with science and rheumatology.

In a humorous essay about his father's habits of economy, Christopher ridiculed how his father once bought a good second-hand car, but admitted having copied most of his father's economies. In fact, living in Costa Rica, where taxis are very cheap, he manages without a car.

Charles was scrupulously honest in all things. He calculated our income tax before the apartment building made that job too time-consuming. In fact, before the IRS took tax out of dividends before the company paid the stockholders, he always declared and paid tax on these dividends, when 80 percent of the stockholders did not. For this reason the government began taking the tax before investors got their hands on it. Still, we were audited several times, but they never got any more money from us, not even when they took us to court and Charles, without a lawyer, defended us and beat the IRS to a draw, on the taxes he had prepared himself.

❋

Charles's intelligence was immediately apparent, not just from the usual criteria of report cards and scholarships (at a time when scholarships went to real "scholars"): being valedictorian in high school; winning a four-year scholarship by competitive examination in his county; graduating with a BS with high honors from college; being accepted in the world's premier medical school; having an IQ sufficient to qualify him for Mensa (top 2 percent).

His contribution to nutritional studies in healthy young men resulted in his being grandfathered into the newly organized American Board of Nutrition. The Walter Reed Army Museum recognized his work by requesting a portrait for their collection of 400 medical scientists, going back to the sixteenth century. Finally, his second place in the Carol Nachman international competition acknowledged his leadership in rheumatology. Other indicators of Charles's high intelligence include a memory that not only made him a consistent winner in quizzes such as Trivial Pursuit, and specialty quizzes such as the one slanted to people of Polish heritage; it was also obvious from his interesting fund of knowledge and conversational abilities on most subjects. Another way his intelligence was displayed was seeing connections between two widely separated facts, e.g., his recognition that the fact that aspirin makes red blood cells slippery could make aspirin a preventative treatment for heart attack or stroke, both caused by clumping of red cells that cannot slip through small or large arteries. He took this idea to the chairman of the cardiology department, who replied,

"What do you know, you're not a cardiologist!" Had Charles's observation been heeded, aspirin treatment could have been introduced earlier as an accepted treatment.

Another sign of high intelligence is called "thinking outside the box," or imagining different, improved ways of doing things. When he needed technicians to help with his ^{35}S work on rats, he did not look for help among technicians trained in the many procedures used to benefit patients either diagnostically or therapeutically. He needed persons of high intelligence who could be trained in the methods used in research with rats as test animals: to handle rats, draw blood or inject test materials into their tail veins, prepare their tissues for study, and maintain all radioactive precautions. He found these characteristics in middle-aged women whose children no longer required full-time attention and who wished to perform worthwhile and interesting work rather than play bridge with their friends. He respected their service and rewarded it by putting their names on papers.

Charles was a lifetime student, spending half a day a week at the "new journals table" in the library to scan anything thought or proven in the field of rheumatology, and many related discoveries, some of which he would recall and use in another connection years later. His students often, years later, would comment, "His lecture twenty-five years ago was the first time I ever heard about ________." Charles thought that everyone in attendance (students, professors, researchers) was like himself and began each lecture wherever he gave it, "Good morning, fellow students." Not long before he left the university to complete, with Malemud's help, organization of his data for publication, a young woman in the hall asked him, "Are you the Doctor Denko who studied nutrition in conscientious objectors in World War 2? We study your papers in my class."

Charles was a "problem-solver" par excellence. He used this term frequently, including when he was teaching the children principles of intelligent thought. It is of interest that, after our sons had left home but visited, each of the three independently credited their father: "He made me a problem-solver."

Another facet of high intelligence is the ability to handle personal finances wisely, saving and investing, while not devoting an entire life to it. He estimated that he spent an hour a week keeping track of our finances, usually on Wednesday evening when I was at Great Books. Charles had a delightful sense of humor. His wit was clever but gentle, never sarcastic or hurtful. He was twice voted the most humorous man in the class, in high school and again in college.

❈

Charles was blessed with a long and healthy life. Having completed his formal education by graduating from medical school at thirty-five, he began the contributing part of life, which continued actively for more than fifty years, until not long before his death at almost ninety. Few people are as dedicated to their life work as Charles. At home or anywhere else in the world, he was always alert and sympathetic to anything rheumatologic. "What a terrible backache that poor creature [dinosaur skeleton] must have suffered!" Or, "Just look at Eric Sevareid's hands!"

His life was rich with a balance of science and family living. Notice how often he was able to exploit earlier good choices to recoup dividends years later.

He followed his own advice: "Work hard at something important and love it." (While he loved his work, this did not keep him from enjoying other things, such as the beauty of nature and the fascinating animals we observed in the wild.)

Charles's motto echoes Teddy Roosevelt's famous dictum: "Far and away the best prize that life has to offer is the chance to work hard at work worth doing."

"Is it fair to say that Charles changed the direction of osteo-arthritis research?"

I would state unequivocally yes. Here's why: Prior to his experimental studies, there wasn't really any consideration that inflammation played a critical role in driving osteoarthritis (OA). However, based on the results of the studies he and his colleagues performed in the Scott Lab at Fairview Hospital and then here at University Hospitals, that was about to change. First, the idea that the hypothalamic-pituitary axis was involved in OA was not even on the radar screen before the growth hormone (Gh)/IGF-1 results were published in the early 1990s. I think it was in 1994 that Ralleigh W. Moskowitz, M.D., first announced the compilation of results regarding the role of GH/IGF-1 in driving OA at a meeting in Val David, Canada. (I recall sitting in the audience waiting for RWM to praise Chuck for altering our thinking about OA at the time, but as you know now, that was not to be.) However, when Chuck and I had the opportunity to discuss these issues further, I began to consider that the OA paradigm had changed from being merely a focal degeneration of the synovial joint to a progressive systemic disorder involving, of course, GH/IGF-1 but also other mediators of inflammation. We first went out on a limb when we published the paper describing OA as a "systemic metabolic disturbance."[1] The rest is history. OA is now considered to be composed of a final common pathway with overlapping similarities to that of rheumatoid arthritis.[2]

It is also safe to say that interactions with Chuck surely changed the trajectory of my career in OA research. [3,4] Finally, I feel that I'm on safe ground when I say that this groundbreaking experimental and clinical research led by your husband changed OA research forever!

1 Denko, CW, Malemud CJ: Metabolic disturbances and synovial joint responses in osteoarthritis. Front Biosci 4: d686-d693, 1999.

2 Malemud, CJ, Shulte ME: Is there a final pathway for arthritis? Future Rheumatol 3: 253-268, 2008.

3 Denko, CW, Malemud CJ: Role of the growth hormone/insulin-like growth factor-1 paracrine axis in rheumatic diseases. Semin Arthritis Rheum 35: 24-34, 2005.

4 Malemud CJ: The biological basis of osteoarthritis: State of the evidence. Curr Opin Rheumatol 27: 289-294, 2015.

Acknowledgments

I am grateful to Sal Glynn for his help in converting my biography of Charles into a form appropriate for young adults. He also added a number of historical references and quotations that enriched the content appreciably. I thank Joe Shaw and Cynthia Frank for their usual patience with my many changes. Finally, I am indebted to my friend Charles Grace for his summary of Charles as a role model whom we all would do well to follow.